THE GLOUCESTERSHIRE WAY

A 100 mile walk through Gloucestershire of
'Forest and vale and high blue hill'

Designed and Compiled by Gerry Stewart
Illustrations by Genny Proctor

COUNTRYSIDE MATTERS

First published in 1996 by
COUNTRYSIDE MATTERS
15 Orchard Road
Alderton
Tewkesbury
Gloucestershire   GL20 8NS

Typeset by Ex Libris Press
Bradford on Avon, Wiltshire

Printed and bound by Cromwell Press
Broughton Gifford, Melksham

ISBN 0 9527870 0 8

Contents

Acknowledgements

I should like to acknowledge the early pioneers from Tewkesbury Walking Club. Their enthusiasm for the diversity of the Gloucestershire Way, and the accompanying poetry, was mainly responsible for my continued interest in completing this guidebook.

Later guinea pigs included members of Cleeve Ramblers, whose chairman, Brenda Murphy, provides the evocative description of the early walks, in her Foreword.

Additionally, many friends have assisted either by commenting on the text, assisting with last minute checks or by their general encouragement. Kate's forebearance, particularly during the final drafting, has been exemplary. Hopefully her fortitude, having walked the Gloucestershire Way on five occasions to date, has not weakened and she will walk it with me again.

Finally, I was very thankful when my mass of notes was transformed by a word processor. Genny Proctor was my saviour, instructing and coaxing me in the intricacies of desk top publishing whilst carrying out most of the labour involved herself. Most of the illustrations were also her work although the cover design was very much a joint effort.

Credits

The publishers wish to thank the following for their kind permission in allowing the use of the following poems to illustrate the Gloucestershire Way.

Patrick Flower and the Lilliput Press for *Forest of Dean*, by Robin Flower.

The Literary Executor of Leonard Clark for *Cider House,* from *The Way It Was.*

Andrew Dalby for *Roel Gate* by Arthur Dalby.

Penny Ely, Trustee of the Gurney Estate, for *East Wind, Up There* and *Near Mid-Summer* by Ivor Gurney from *The Collected Poems of Ivor Gurney.*

Patrick Harvey for *A Song of Gloucestershire, In Flanders* and *Spring 1924* by F W Harvey, from *A Gloucestershire Lad at Home and Abroad.*

Clarissa Mitchel and the Gloucestershire Special Adventure Playground Association for *Cotswold Tiles* by Edward Berryman, from *Nursery Rhymes of Gloucestershire.*

Author's note

Other than several short lengths of quiet roads, The Gloucestershire Way is entirely on public rights of way, mainly footpaths and bridleways. However, changes continually take place in the countryside, hedges disappear, new fences, sometimes without stiles, arise and paths may become difficult to follow through crops. Additionally, public rights of way are subject to legal diversions which may not be reflected in current maps. County Council signposting should reveal these changes but the situation may not always be clear on the ground.

Whilst every possible care has been taken to ensure that the information provided in this guidebook is accurate, neither the author nor publisher can accept responsibility for any errors or omissions, or for the interpretation placed on the information by user's of the guidebook.

The unresolved national issues concerning metrication had placed me in a dilemma. Advice from the Long Distance Paths Association suggested that both metric and imperial units could be employed, statutory miles being quoted for longer distances and metrication used for shorter distances. This seemed to work satisfactorily, until having to decide if 1.5 kilometres should be 1500 metres or three-quarters of a mile. Also, describing the prominent tower of Gloucester Cathedral as 68.58 metres in height seemed singularly inappropriate.

Fortunately, assistance arrived in the form of *The Units of Measurements Regulations 1995*. This advises that imperial units of measurement may remain in use for traffic signs and related distances for the forseeable future, and I have taken this at face value and retained familiar miles, yards and feet throughout.

The maps are reduced from the O.S.6 inch series. They should be more than adequate for the walk, including the diversions offered and the many alternative routes. Although the royalties have considerably added to production costs the savings against purchasing eight Pathfinder maps for the route are very worthwhile. Visitors to Gloucestershire may find it helpful to obtain the smaller scale Landranger maps for an overall view of the countryside of the Gloucestershire Way. Better still perhaps, the Outdoor Leisure Map for the Wye Valley and Forest of Dean and the O.S. Tourist Map to the Cotswolds enhance a leisurely approach to the walk.

Any serious problem encountered on The Gloucestershire Way should be reported either to the Police, who are responsible for such matters as dangerous dogs and wheeled vehicles on all highways, or to the County Council's Public Rights of Way Unit, Shire Hall, Gloucester, who are responsible for the signposting and condition of public rights of way.

Foreword

I am glad that I was able to join Gerry and Kate Stewart's exploratory walks along the Gloucestershire Way during 1993, particularly so as this is the route finally published here. The Gloucestershire Way is very much Gerry's baby. Being a country-lover, interested in local history and folklore and knowledgeable about those who have written about such things, the route was directly influenced by local poets, particularly Ivor Gurney of Gloucester and Will Harvey of Minsterworth, who provide the theme of 'Forest and vale and high blue hill'.

The 100 mile walk begins in Chepstow, runs north east through the Forest of Dean to the Severn at Gloucester and then crosses the Vale north of Gloucester, through the Golden Valley, climbs up into the Cotswolds to Stow-on-the-Wold and doubles back through Winchcombe to finish in Tewkesbury. For our purposes the walk was divided into eight sections, spread over four weekends - March, June, September and November and it promised to be a wonderfully varied walk through all four seasons. What more could anyone ask? The linear nature of the walk necessitated a minibus ferrying us either at the beginning or the end of each day's stage and each ride added to the enjoyment.

It would take too much space to recount in detail the whole walk, but certain places and events stand out in my memory.

I remember well the bright, sunny start at Chepstow in March, the keen breeze and steady pull up out of the town onto the hill where we got our first superb views of the Severn Bridge rising elegantly into the bright blue sky. Across the Severn, the long sweep of the eastern bank, from Oldbury Power Station and beyond up through Sharpness and Berkeley, the narrow deep water channel clearly visible, fighting for survival between the treacherous mud banks and flats. The Cotswolds look a long way off from here, definitely an exciting challenge.

FOREWORD

The footpaths and narrow, winding lanes were bathed in glorious sunshine and the hedgerows full of the joys of Spring. We finished in Parkend that first day, towards the southerly end of the Forest. The second day - Parkend to May Hill – over hill and down dale, through the heart of the lovely Forest of Dean, full of interest, changing vistas, contrasts and surprises, full of history, yet a living, working place. The weather was not quite so kind to us and we finished the day clambering up the steepest side of May Hill in a fine drizzle to reach the summit clump of pines, a landmark to be seen for miles around.

Three months on, June, from forest to vale at Minsterworth, home of W H Harvey, local poet, and then on to Gloucester, cathedral city of the Shire via Telford's Bridge and parkland avoiding the noisy traffic along Over Causeway. Good weather for this low level trek across the plain, avoiding the built-up areas nicely; Sandhurst, Down Hatherley, Staverton Airfield, where we lunched and exchanged greetings with passing aircraft pilots; long grass, briar roses, damsel flies and skylarks; summer it surely was. Badgeworth Church made a drinks stop memorable, as a peep inside was rewarded with the sight of beautiful floral arrangements for a recent wedding. Another climb to finish this leg, this time up to Birdlip, out of the Vale and onto the 'high blue hill'.

The September stage took us eventually to Stow-on-the-Wold via Salperton, a lovely sleepy, hidden hamlet, alive with pheasants at this Autumn time. Quietly undulating, easy walking through narrow lanes, stubble fields and little villages with ancient names - Notgrove, Cold Aston and Lower Slaughter. The breeze was chill now, and the sky had that pale blue far-away look, but there is nothing better than the Cotswolds at this time of the year. I saw my first kingfisher in flight, skimming the surface of the River Dickler. The poplars and whitebeams were showing their silver backs - autumn was well on the way.

The last stage, and almost the back-end of the year now; Stow to Tewkesbury by way of Condicote, Winchcombe, Oxenton and Walton Cardiff. Langley and Woolstone Hills just providing that bit of challenge and the biting facing winds making it uncomfortable for a while. But

9

the end was in sight .... the Abbey tower of Tewkesbury. Later I hear talk of a further stage to connect to the Worcestershire Way.... and the Malvern Hills seem to beckon strangely in the background!)

Brenda Murphy, Chairman
Cleeve Group, Ramblers Association

Introduction

Over the years we have enjoyed many long distance walks and these gave the necessary impetus to devise some of our own. One memorable journey was an autumn week walking back to Ribblesdale after taking the train to Carlisle on the splendid Settle - Ribblehead line. There have been many similar.

A weekend of particularly enjoyable walking arose out of the renowned Three Choirs Festival at Gloucester. This festival has taken place for over 250 years alternating between the cathedral cities of Hereford, Worcester and Gloucester. A group of appreciative walkers from Tewkesbury Walking Club had previously enjoyed walking weekends with literary and musical themes at Hereford and Worcester respectively. We were asked to complete the trilogy by arranging an itinerary of walks centred on a visit to a concert at Gloucester Cathedral. The resulting walks, partly in the Forest of Dean and partly on Cotswold, together with a relevant theme of local poetry and prose, were so well received that the seeds of The Gloucestershire Way were sown.

It was decided to pass through as many parishes as possible to encourage local affinity for the Way using the local path network and to emphasise the connecting thread between the diverse areas of Dean, Vale and Cotswold. Although the Severn dictates the choice of route, the ancient river crossing at Gloucester provides a focal point for the journey. Views of the Cathedral tower across the river and vale emphasising the transition from Dean to Cotswold. During the winter months the footpaths on either side of the river at Gloucester are liable to flooding, when a route along the main roads might become necessary for short distances. However, many, particularly local walkers, will be surprised at the pleasant green corridor between Gloucester and Cheltenham to gain the Cotswold scarp at Crickley.

The Way conveniently breaks down into stages and it has proved popular to complete the walk during four or more weekends over the year, the effect of walking through the seasons adding greatly to the enjoyment. Although many will no doubt follow the route described, there are often variations available to suit personal preference. The Gloucestershire Way can also be utilised for short day walks with many alternative paths available to provide circular walks. A large percentage of day walkers will use car transport to the start of a route taking in the Gloucestershire Way. In most villages there is reasonable parking, often with a pub or shop available. Exceptions are in the vicinity of May Hill and Salperton where parking needs a little care and planning.

I have described the walk starting from Chepstow to avoid walking into the prevailing weather, usually from the south west. However, the direction of travel is a matter of choice and there is the added convenience that the walk can be joined at many points along the way.

Being a hundred miles long, The Gloucestershire Way is a worthwhile path for the increasing number of people who take pleasure from following a long continuous route on foot. It will also appeal to many walkers, from both home and abroad, who will appreciate the convenient manner in which the Way joins several other long distance paths. A valuable link is also provided between established and planned National Trails, and will create a chain of many hundreds of miles of countryside walking. This should be of considerable benefit to local rural economies.

Bus timetables are available from Gloucestershire County Council, although these may not be very helpful and it may be more convenient to use taxis or mini-buses to the start or the end of the days walk. This has been found to be both efficient and economical for completing The Gloucestershire Way in stages. Accommodation lists can be obtained from Gloucester City Council and the respective District Councils for the Forest of Dean, Cotswolds and Tewkesbury (*see Appendix 4*).

This outline of a pleasurable walk through Gloucestershire is not intended as an anthology of poetry or to have artistic merit. Nonetheless, the theme of 'Forest and vale and high blue hill' is very apt, and we have been told by numerous people who have completed the walk, that the poetry has enhanced their journey. There have been many local musicians and poets who have emphasised the pleasures of the Gloucestershire countryside through their works. In recent years the Poets Paths and the Daffodil Way near Newent provide examples of the popularity of literary reference to walking.

The theme for the Gloucestershire Way was suggested from *Poems of Gloucestershire, the Cotswolds and Beyond*, an anthology of local poets compiled by musician Johnny Coppin and published by The Windrush Press. This was extremely helpful in revealing some of the wonderful material directly relating to the Gloucestershire countryside. In this guidebook the poems have been chosen to enhance the particular route and many popular local poets, Laurie Lee, Frank Mansell and others, are excluded as their work just didn't happen to fit the twists and turns of the walk.

The Gloucestershire Way is a memorable ramble through varied countryside, likely to appeal to many types of walkers, including families. Mainly on field and woodland paths, usually maintained in excellent condition and well signposted by Gloucestershire County Council.

This is truly a walk for all seasons.

Gerry and Kate Stewart, April 1996.

A Song of Gloucestershire

(dedicated to the Glos. Society)

North, South, East, and West:
Think of whichever you love the best.
Forest and vale and high blue hill:
You may have whicheveryou will,
And quaff one cup to the love o' your soul
Before we drink to the lovely whole.

Here are high hills with towns all stone,
(Did you come from the Cotswolds then?)
And an architecture all their own,
And a breed of sturdy men.

But here's a forest old and stern,
(Say, do you know the Wye?)
Where sunlight dapples green miles of fern,
A river wandering by.

Here's peaceful meadow-land and kine,
(Do you see a fair grey tower?)
Where sweet together close entwine
Grass, clover, and daisy flower.

Here stretches the land towards the sea,
(Behold the castle bold!)
Where men live out life merrily,
And die merry and old.

North, South, East, and West:
Think of whichever you love the best.
Forest and vale and high blue hill:
You may have whicheveryou will,
And quaff one cup to the love o' your soul
Before we drink to the lovely whole.

                                        F W Harvey

Chepstow to Parkend

Being a true border crossing, bridges are important to Chepstow. The last Roman bridge, close to the Castle, lasted for hundreds of years until the Normans constructed a timber bridge in the 13th Century. This was replaced by subsequent bridges until the last became rotten and dangerous in 1810 when John Rennie, designer of London Bridge, was hired to oversee repairs. Instead he recommended a new bridge and the present structure was built to his design by John Rastrick of Bridgnorth. This bridge, opened in 1816, was the only crossing from Gloucestershire for an increasing volume and weight of traffic until 1988 when the new bypass and road bridge were opened. Today only light traffic is permitted on the old Wye Bridge.

> *The 70 miles long 'Wye Valley Walk' commences near the Castle and follows the beautiful Wye Valley to Tintern, and then the meandering river past Monmouth, Ross-on-Wye and Hereford to reach Hay-on-Wye deep into the Welsh Marches.*

Chepstow, 'a market place at a river crossing', dominated since the 11th Century by the massive Castle alongside the Wye, is a splendidly positioned and atmospheric place for the beginning, or end, of a walk such as this.

Leave Chepstow by the old Wye Bridge, where the centre panel indicates the boundary between England and Wales, and walk up the lane directly ahead (Old Hill). Half-way up, Offas' Dyke National Trail joins from an alley on the right. Cross the road at the top and continue up Mopla Road, passing a signpost where the National Trail branches to follow the Wye Valley northward.

> *The Offa's Dyke National Trail was opened in 1971 and follows closely the great earth work built to the order of Offa the powerful King of Mercia in the 8th Century. The trail is 168 miles of splendid walking along the Welsh Border between Chepstow and Prestatyn on the North Wales Coast. The National Trail connects The Shropshire Way (172 miles) at Clun and Glyndwr's Way (120 miles) at Knighton.*

At the next road junction, continue straight ahead, for about 150 yards before turning right into Elm Road to a footpath on the left within 25 yards. This path is narrow and sometimes overgrown but soon leads to a stone stile of local red sandstone, and the first open view of the River Severn with the blue Cotswold scarp beyond. Cross fields to Bishton Lane and beyond to Bishton Farm, with a widening view of the Severn estuary over your right shoulder. Cross two stiles to pass behind the farm and turn left on the track uphill. Through a gate and follow the boundary of the field to the right and then as it bends left to join a narrow lane at a further gate. Turn left for about 200 yards to a footpath on the left and walk alongside the disused railway line to Netherhope.

The Chepstow to Monmouth Railway was closed in 1958 as being unprofitable. There has been a recent private feasibility study on the re-opening of the line for tourism but this is unlikely to take place due to the expense involved. It has been rumoured that the line might be reopened if extensive stone quarrying were permitted. The tunnel is walkable but this is not advocated. Certainly, whatever happens the line should be preserved for its immense amenity value.

Crossing Netherhope Lane, where the railway line disappears underground, take the green lane between the cottages and walk up the attractive dell to reach a stile and open fields. Cross to the corner of the hedge line where the public footpath enters the next field by a gate hidden from view as you approach. Unfortunately this path is usually impassable, because of slurry flowing from the farm buildings. At the time of publication Gloucestershire County Council have advised that a diversion of the path, to the right hand side of the hedge, is being processed. It is advisable to follow this route to a stile. Walk up the next field, to a further stile and then through a garden to a stone slab stile onto a track.

Turn right to a road and follow this downhill to a junction, keep left and after a few yards turn left into a green lane. Follow this uphill to a gate and continue with the hedge on the right to a gate and stile.

Pause for breath and take in the view behind which extends from the heights of Chepstow in a wide arc over the lower Severn estuary and vale to the Cotswold scarp beyond. Cross the stile and walk up through scrub and gorse, with a fence on the left, to another stile into woodland. Beyond, take the right fork in the path and in about 200 yards cross over a track. *A short distance off to the right a tall monolith recording the Jubilee of Queen Victoria can be found and which is a pleasant spot to stop for refreshment.* From this slight elevation views open up of the Severn Vale and the hills as far north as Gloucester. The rising ground of the forest gives the line of the Gloucestershire Way ahead. Continuing, cross a second green track and walk down to a lane and cottage at Ashgrove.

From the cottage continue straight over and slightly downhill on another lane. As this climbs ignore a track to the left and continue to the right to pass a white cottage after a short distance. Where the lane bends sharply right continue ahead on a green path through undergrowth and a coppice.

Follow the edge of the next field down to another lane at Ashwell Grove and continue directly over this to a path through woodland. After crossing a forest track the woodland path joins a lane near a small barn. Turn left for about 160 yards to find a path on the right which climbs slightly around the top of old quarried ground to a stile into woodland. The path is sometimes overgrown but follows close to the left hand boundary. The exit from the wood is down the slope to the right and through a gap alongside metal fencing and a gate in the corner.

Continue along the edge of a pleasant meadow and pass through a second metal gate. Turn half right and descend to a further corner where a stile, hidden from view as you approach, gives access onto an old green track. Follow this downhill and turn right through a gate, ignoring a stile and gate straight ahead. About 100 yards along the length of enclosed track climb over a stile on the left and descend a hollow path. At the bottom of the slope walk to the right and follow the farm track up the contour to reach Slade Farm. A barn has been extended over the track and a path has been created around the right hand side of the barn. Follow the farm track pleasantly down to join a road at a sharp bend. From the bend follow the track climbing up to the left through woodland, before levelling out to give sweeping views. *To the south, beyond the two Severn bridges, are the 'Kings Roads' the old sailing ship anchorage off Avonmouth. To the east, and perhaps not so interesting, are Berkeley and Oldbury power stations. Further north lie Sharpness Docks and, in good visibility, Robinswood Hill beyond Gloucester.*

When the track joins a road this is followed down to the right. At a sharp right bend take a footpath off to the left, over a stile and descend a pleasant track curving left under oak and beech trees. The track levels and continues to some ruined buildings where the route can be ambiguous, sometimes boggy and overgrown by bracken. Leave the track and turn half right through an old orchard to a gateway, and follow this line to a further gate onto an enclosed track.

Follow this to the right to a lane, turn left and shortly cross a stream and then a crossroad. Continue straight on for about quarter of a mile before turning right onto a public footpath into Clanna Wood. Follow the path down to the sluice. *It is well worth deviating off to the right for a few minutes to a tranquil lake in a woodland setting. An ideal spot for rest and refreshment on The Gloucestershire Way.*

Resuming from the sluice, ignore the forest tracks curving off left and right and take the path straight ahead up the slope. At a junction with a track fork right past Wood Cottage, and take the path immediately to the left, descending through a green tunnel to a stile over a stream. The path curves to the right across a field to reach a gate and the road. Turn right down to the next bend, about 100 yards, and turn into the forest track to the left. This forks within a few yards and The Gloucestershire Way follows the right branch through mature woodland.

The paths and tracks through the forest are subject to forestry operations and otherwise firm tracks may become badly churned when felling takes place. This is adequately compensated for by the many other pleasant tracks and paths available. Access generally throughout the forest is more often than not a pleasant exercise.

A stile denotes the boundary between the parishes of St Briavels and Alvington, and beyond this the path winds gently uphill for half a mile through mature woodland where masses of foxgloves bloom in summer. The path comes close to a stream and passes a pond before entering an enclosed dell where path and stream intertwine for a short distance. After crossing two stiles a diversion of the public right of way takes an attractive line to the left around two lakes. Climb up to a stile onto a farm track and turn right.

At the farm buildings the public path turns right and then immediately left to reach the road at Round House. Turn left for a few yards to a stile on the right. Walk up the sloping field to a stile on the horizon and continue up the slope to the highest point on the route so far, about 650 feet above sea level. *The extensive views ahead include the villages of Clearwell and Sling to the left, Little Drybrook and Bream directly ahead and closer, with Whitecroft and Yorkley further away to the right.*

From the high ground the path angles down to the left to a gate in the corner of the field, hidden by the contour. From the gate continue on the same angle, down a long field, to a gate in the bottom corner and concealed from view until the last moment by a hawthorn tree. Turn left on the road but just short of a road junction take a path to the right, alongside the hedge away from the busy road. After 100 yards climb the embankment and follow the verge before crossing the road to a track along the edge of a disused quarry. This track curves right to cross a road and then follows a narrow lane lined with cottages downhill.

Hereabouts is the boundary of the ancient Dean Forest (see Appendix 1).

Where the lane turns sharply right, take the green path straight ahead, again downhill. This contours down under power lines and across a stream by a small footbridge to join a rough stone track serving the scattered houses. Descend further to cross over a road and down the grass slope beyond, cutting across the bend in the road.

Turn left up a grassy ramp, but ignore the stile into the forest and instead turn right along an enclosed green track. Follow this, firstly level and then descending slightly, at the edge of mature conifers to a track crossing from the factory buildings on the right. Turn left up to a stile and track and cross directly over on a path through the trees to join a track descending to the right. Where this shortly bends to the left take a path off to the right, descending through larch and silver birch to a stile and another forest track.

Turn right to a junction and without crossing the stream take the track cutting back to the left. After 60 yards this track forks and The Gloucestershire Way follows the right hand branch along a well drained green track. After a short distance this climbs away from the valley bottom through young oak, beech and Scots pine and the occasional holly tree.

Cross a level green ride and walk up for a few yards to a gravelled forest road. Turn right uphill for a short distance before descending to reach the Coleford - Parkend road. Cross this to the lane behind the cottages and follow this curving uphill to cross the old railway track. *Now an amenity route, this can be followed, to the right, into Parkend, where there are pubs, a shop and overnight accommodation.*

The Forest of Dean

The quiet congregation of the trees
Awoke to a rippled whisper. The light winged breeze
Brushed leaf against leaf; softly and delicately fingering
Silken beech and ragged oak leaf; and in the cool shadow
And wavering dapple of tremulous sunlight lingering
As weary of the hot glow of the buttercup meadow,
And renewing his strength in the cool green and still shade
Of the forest, deeper and deeper burrowing in
By pathway and trackway and green ride and arched glade
Over hyacinth and the white starred garlic and curled fern,
And dreaming in some unvisited haven to win
New life from the growing grass and rejoicing return
To sweep from hill to valley, from valley to hill.

Robin Flowers

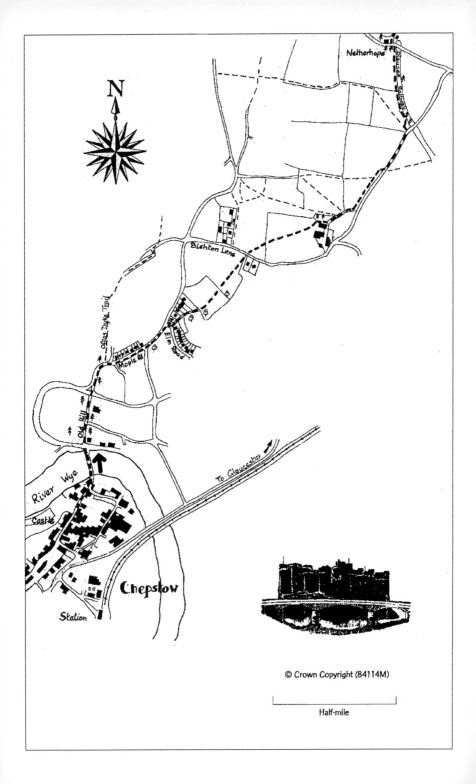

N

Netherhope

Bishton Lane

Offa's Dyke Trail

Elm Road

Maple St

Old Hill

To Gloucester

River Wye

Castle

Chepstow

Station

© Crown Copyright (84114M)

Half-mile

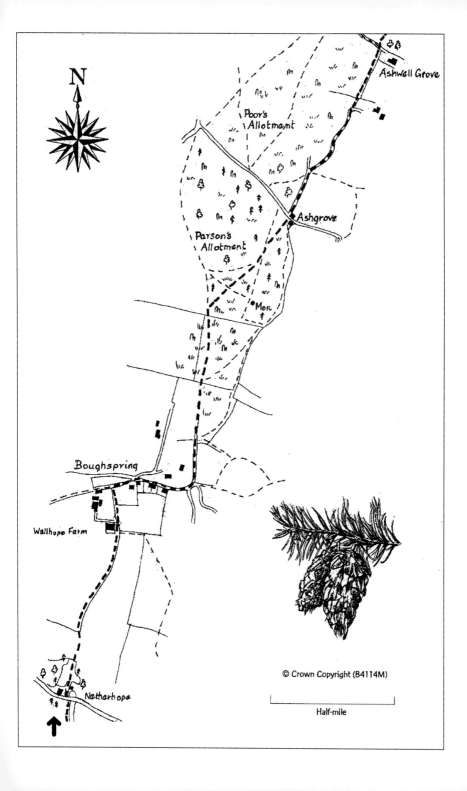

N

Ashwell Grove

Poor's
Allotment

Ashgrove

Parson's
Allotment

Mon.

Boughspring

Wallhope Farm

Netherhope

© Crown Copyright (84114M)

Half-mile

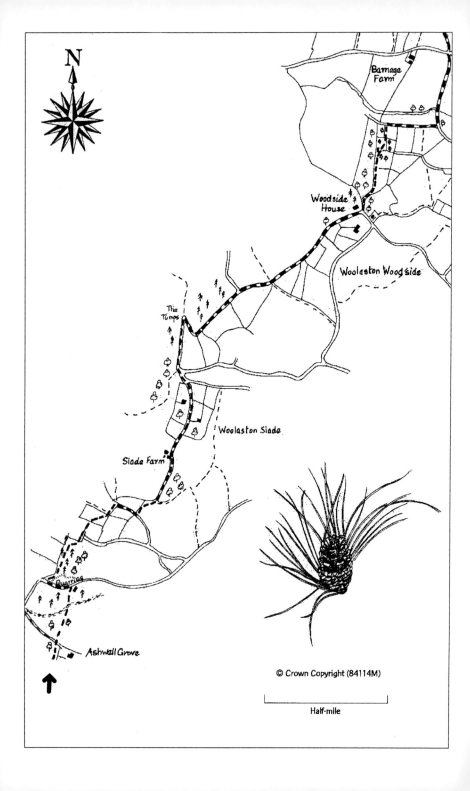

N

Barnage
Farm

Woodside
House

Woolaston Woodside

The
Tumps

Woolaston Slade

Slade Farm

Quarries

Ashwell Grove

© Crown Copyright (84114M)

Half-mile

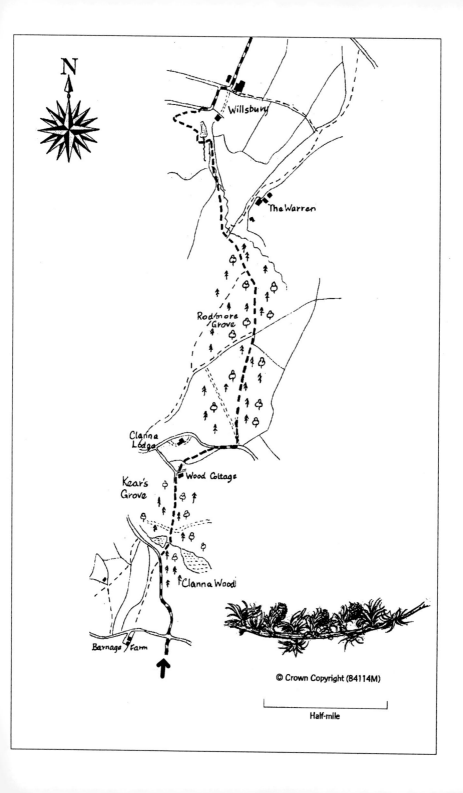

N

Willsbury

The Warren

Rodmore
Grove

Clanna
Lodge

Wood Cottage

Kear's
Grove

Clanna Wood

Barnage Farm

© Crown Copyright (84114M)

Half-mile

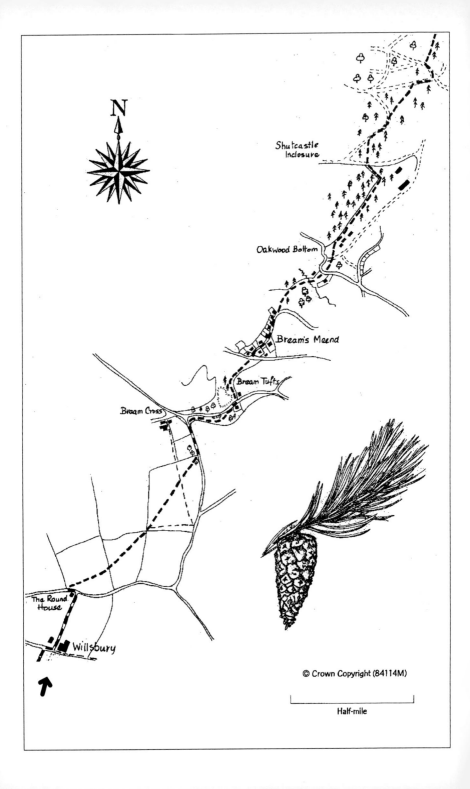

N

Shutcastle
Inclosure

Oakwood Bottom

Bream's Meend

Bream Tufts

Bream Cross

The Round
House

Willsbury

© Crown Copyright (84114M)

Half-mile

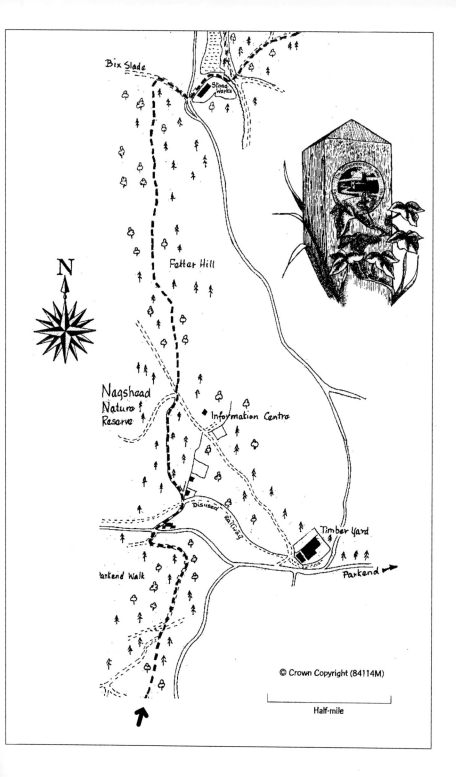

N

Bix Slade

Stone Works

Fetter Hill

Nagshead
Nature
Reserve

Information Centre

Disused railway

Timber Yard

Parkend Walk

Parkend →

© Crown Copyright (84114M)

Half-mile

Parkend to May Hill

Immediately after crossing the old railway ignore the track to the right alongside the buildings and instead take the waymarked green path to the left. Where this path meets the access track to Nags Head Nature Reserve, cross over and follow the right hand of two paths leading into the forest ahead. Follow this pleasant line through the forest under young oak and beech to descend gradually to a final gate and stile onto the line of the old tramway from Bixslade quarry. The stone sleepers set into this track show indentations where the fishplates were drilled into the stone. Turn right down to the road and cross over to follow the boundary fence of the Stone works to the sluice at Cannop Ponds.

Stone has always been extensively quarried in Dean. Building stone was mainly old red sandstone, Drybrook sandstone and Pennant sandstone from the Coal Measures, which is often shaded grey, blue or red. Examples of Pennant stone can be seen in Telford's Bridge at Over crossed later on the Gloucestershire Way, and at Eastnor Castle, which can be seen from the link between The Gloucestershire Way and Worcestershire Way.

As a result of steam power Parkend became a centre of the stone trade in the 19th century when stone troughs and cider presses became a major product.

Alternative route:
Over the dam, the attractive path alongside the ponds provides a short alternative route for The Gloucestershire Way. Turn left and walk to the end of the first pond, where there is an area of marsh. On the right at this point is a car parking area with a footpath leading uphill alongside the course of a tumbling stream. On reaching a stile turn left on the forest track and rejoin The Gloucestershire Way.

From the sluice walk to the right and cross the line of another old railway, now converted into an all-weather horse and cycle trail. Go through a gate on the left and follow a waymarked track leading gently uphill away from the ponds. At the first cross tracks encountered turn left through pleasant mixed woodland. Pass the next track on the right and shortly afterwards cross a stream, where the alternative route from Cannop Ponds rejoins via the stile on the left.

Walk up the slope and turn right onto the next track. Within a short distance cross a further track and climb more steeply to reach a junction of five tracks. Ignore the track to the left and continue straight over. At the next junction take the left fork and continue for about 400 yards or so to a stile. Cross this and follow the track curving left. Take the next right turn, without reaching the road, under huge oaks mixed with holly, to reach Speech House.

The original forest covered a much larger extent than we see today, roughly the area between Chepstow, Ross-on-Wye, Newent and Highnam. Powerful landowners extracted areas of Tidenham and Hewelsfield parishes and large tracts of land became deforested. The remaining forest was a popular resort of Norman kings who gave the Constable of St Briavels Castle the additional jobs of Head Keeper of the Forest and also President of the Mine Law Court. Under the Keepership the forest was divided into ten bailiwicks, in an effort to protect the forest against encroachment by farming, mining and, particularly, the iron smelting which consumed vast quantities of timber.

These encroachments became so serious that the remaining forest was enclosed in 1667 and declared free of all common rights. The bailiwicks were replaced by six Forest Walks each with its own Lodge for an appointed Keeper. The King's Lodge or Speech House became the Court of the forest where most business of the Verderers and Freeminers was transacted. Visitors to Speech House should note the shield over the western entrance which once bore the date 1630. Even if not dining it will probably be possible to view the old Courtroom at quiet times (see Appendix 1).

Leaving Speech House cross the road and descend the grass bank, ignoring the small gate to the left. Turn right to walk through the woodland and the picnic area below the car park areas. This can be very busy on summer weekends and Bank Holidays. Leaving the picnic area bear left to cross a stile and a major forest track, continue straight over on a similar track.

The track crossed is part of a Sculpture trail and if time permits a visit could be made to part of this at nearby Kemsley Lodge, to see the exhibit 'The Cathedral in the Forest'. The whole route of about four miles takes a couple of hours if all the sculptures are to be enjoyed.

The Forest of Dean Sculpture Project was established in 1986 by the Arnolfini Gallery, Bristol in collaboration with the Forestry Commission. On completion there were 18 exhibits along a four-mile long 'sculpture trail' around Speech House. Some were transient works, constructed from living trees and saplings, others were equally subtle and fragile, none of which have lasted. Many of the permanent works are extremely attractive in the forest setting and readily heighten the sense of history of the forest which can be found in some of the remaining quiet places.

After approximately 400 yards the track turns sharply right and The Gloucestershire Way continues straight on along the grass track with a boundary fence to the left. In another 200 yards ignore a faint track straight ahead and follow the path which bends to the left, past a section of young larch, birch and conifer trees. The path dips down the contours crossing another track and, further down, a shallow stream and then climbs through tall stands of mixed woodland to a forest road. Turn right and then left at a T-junction. Cross the bed of an old railway, then turn immediately right along a green track with a boundary fence on the left.

> *The next section of The Gloucestershire Way, as far as May Hill, is also the route of the proposed Three Rivers Way, a long distance path of about 52 miles connecting Offa's Dyke National Trail at Monmouth with The Thames Path at Kemble.*

Continue for about 400 yards until the track converges with the old railway again, keep left for a few yards before turning left uphill. After a short distance cross a forest track and shortly after that, at an obvious bend, follow a path directly uphill to a stile. Beyond this, young conifers cross the path. Cross a second stile and track and continue uphill under sweet chestnut and beech trees, crowning a small hill. Descend the far side, following roughly the line of a sunken pathway to a triangular junction of forest roads. Either cross directly or follow the angle of the roads and continue to an open space adjacent to factory buildings.

A stile and gate on the right lead into Hawkwell Enclosure. Walk under mature oak trees with Cinderford coming into view on the hills to the right and cross a small stream and then a stile in a fence. Continue straight over on a track through tall conifers to a second stile and an area recently thinned and underplanted. The path shortly forks left onto a further track which is followed to a final stile before reaching a road. Turn right for a few yards before crossing to a footpath over open ground.

Pass close to a wayside stone, possibly an old gatepost, and cross a stream to a stile alongside a gate. Turn left and walk behind the cottage to a second stile giving entry to a lawn and garden. The public path angles to the right to pass between the buttresses of an old railway bridge.

Continue on the same line, passing under an avenue of fine oak trees, until a large white house comes into view. Follow the boundary wall to a forest track with a barrier and a massive oak tree on the right. Cross the track and turn half left, passing under more majestic oaks, up to the Gloucester - Monmouth road.

Turn right and cross the road to a forest track and take the right fork within a few paces. Continue uphill to join another track coming in from the left and at the next fork, take the left branch to the top of the slope and another cross track. Continue straight over and follow a pleasant path, edged with beech trees, winding downhill. Cross the line of an old tramway and continue down a path twisting between gorse and bracken to a stile. Emerge into a car parking area and cross this and a lane, to follow another lane down to the road. Cross over and walk steeply down Hazel Hill past the cottages of Plump Hill. *At the left of a junction is an old serving well which supplied the community with its water before this was piped to the houses.*

Where Hazel Hill turns sharply right uphill, continue downhill with a grass bank on the right. The road ends at two private entrances, the left descends steeply and the right climbs. Take the right hand drive but immediately turn left down a grassy footpath. This soon becomes a track leading to an area beside cottages. Bear left to the road and turn left for a few yards to a gate on the right. Follow the track through fields, curving left past a cow shed and continue uphill, keeping left of an obvious field gate, and follow the hedge up to the road. Walk uphill to a junction and fork right into Church Lane, passing the old Bible School Room to reach Abenhall Church. *There is a Victorian post-box set in the churchyard wall, whilst a stone tablet set into the west wall of the church tower depicts miners' and smiths' tools.*

Continue down the road curving right to a footpath which climbs steeply up the bank on the left hand side. Walk uphill alongside an ancient hedgerow with oak, ash, sycamore, holly, elder, hawthorn and several other species. Ponder on these as you puff up the slope. At the next stile angle up to the left of the trees on the horizon. Pausing for breath, look back to the wide view of the Forest of Dean and ahead, over a pond, to May Hill with its crowning summit of pine.

> *I will go climb my little*
> *hill to see*
> *Severn, and Malverns,*
> *May Hill's tiny grove.*
> **Ivor Gurney**

From the pond follow the hedge down to a stile into the wood where the steep descent needs care. At the bottom of the hill turn left on the farm track to Whitmore Farm. Immediately past the first barn on the right, turn right to slant down to a stile. Follow the field down to a gate and cross the next field, half left, to a stile in a hedge. Continue on the same line, and then walk down the field with a hedge on your left to a gate. Descend through the farm buildings to the Gloucester - Monmouth road again. *May Hill can be avoided if necessary, although this would be to miss a highlight of the walk. Alternative paths can be used, which rejoin the main route near Huntley. This 'short cut' would shorten the journey by four miles.*

Alternative route:
Without crossing the road turn right for a few yards, to a footpath which climbs through an orchard. Further paths can be followed for almost a mile to briefly touch the Gloucester - Monmouth road, then a

further mile climbing the hillside through Blaisdon Wood and descending through Little London. After crossing the narrow Blaisdon road, a direct footpath rejoins The Gloucestershire Way south of Huntley.

Cross to a stile and footbridge and climb the steep field beyond. Walk up the next field close to the hedgerow, to a gate in the far corner sometimes hidden from view by bushes. The gate gives access to a green track which leads to a second gate into a paddock and garden. Turn right and follow the drive downhill between houses to a lane. Turn left and after several hunting gates cross another lane and then open fields to a gate onto an attractive narrow lane hung with trees and bushes. Ignore a stile on the left, turn right for a few paces and then left over a footbridge consisting of two large sandstone slabs. *This bridge is sometimes hidden from the lane by the overhanging bushes.* Follow the next field gently uphill to emerge on a track alongside Longhope village school.

Either turn right down the track and left along the village street at the church or, from the school, turn left up the track for about 100 yards and climb the steps up the steep bank to the right. Descend the field diagonally to a stile just before reaching the grey stone boundary wall ahead.

Follow the village street until it joins the Gloucester - Ross road. Follow the left hand pavement for a few yards to the Nags Head Inn, and perhaps a refreshing pint.

From the Nag's Head, cross the road to a stile in the car park and descend the field to a footbridge over a stream. Cross the embankment of the old railway and, from the far stile, angle to the left to a further stile to descend the verge onto the road. Turn right and right again into a narrow lane signposted 'No Through Road'. Walk steeply uphill to a bend and immediately after the second cottage take the steps up the steep bank on the right. A pleasant route zigzags steeply up the hillside to a coppice. Turn right to find a stile hidden under the overhanging trees. Continue over this uphill alongside the boundary hedge and over further stiles to reach Yartleton Lane. Turn left for 20 yards and then right up a narrow track through National Trust land to the tree clad summit of May Hill.

After regaining your breath, you may be tempted to count the summit trees and check the old superstition that a hundredth tree will not grow? As the Celts are said to have worshipped Baal and the Romans their Goddess Maia here, it is not surprising that old superstitions still linger. The celebrations continued in medieval times, and even today various beliefs are sometimes practiced.

From the summit of May Hill survey the dark wooded ridge of Dean and the whole of the rich red vale of the Leadon. Looking north, over Newent, is Dymock where the 'Dymock poets' wrote themselves into fame during their brief stay in the locality immediately before the First World War.

The proposed Three Rivers Way also crosses the summit of May Hill. This is a proposed long distance path of about 52 miles connecting the Thames Path at Kemble with Offa's Dyke National Trail at Monmouth.

The Thames Path National Trail meanders for 163 miles from the source of the river near Kemble in Gloucestershire to the Thames Barrier at Greenwich.

As befits a well known landmark, visible over a wide area, there are spectacular views from the slopes of May Hill. At 972 feet this is the highest point reached on The Gloucestershire Way, although the area between Cutsdean and Ford, further along The Gloucestershire Way, is close to the same height. To the east contemplate the pleasant walking still to be enjoyed before reaching that point.

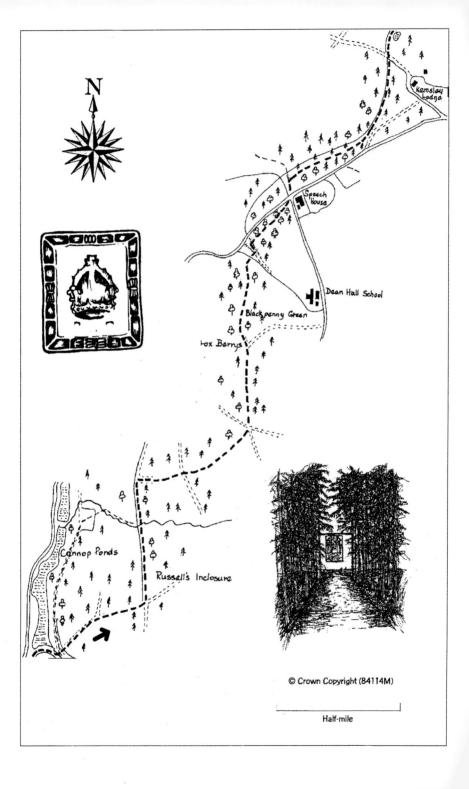

N

Kemsley Lodge

Speech House

Dean Hall School

Blackpenny Green

Fox Barnys

Cannop Ponds

Russell's Inclosure

© Crown Copyright (84114M)

Half-mile

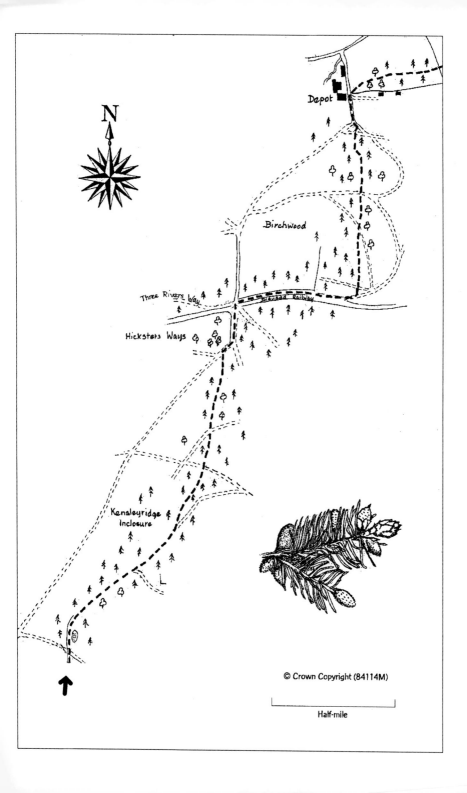

N

Depot

Birchwood

Three Rivers Way

Birchwood Railway

Hicksters Ways

Kensleyridge
Inclosure

© Crown Copyright (84114M)

Half-mile

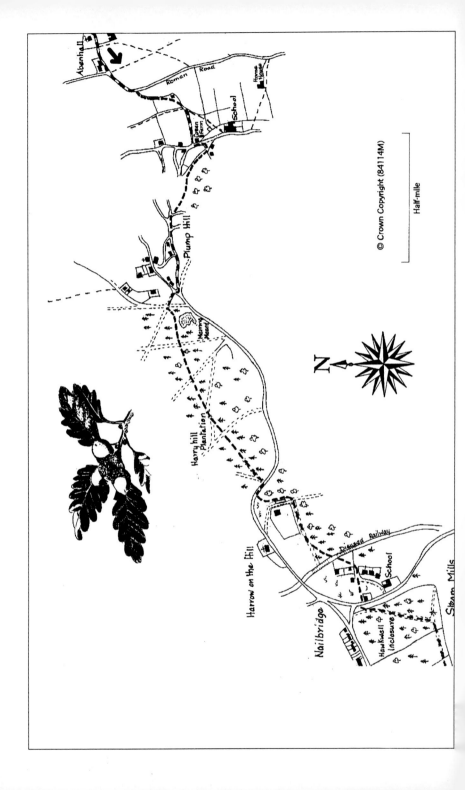

© Crown Copyright (84114M)

Half-mile

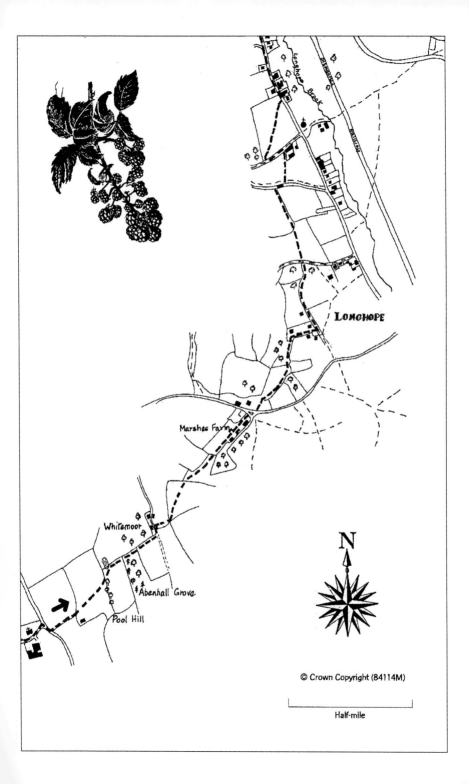

Longhope Brook

RAILWAY

LONGHOPE

Marshes Farm

Whitemoor

Abenhall Grove

Pool Hill

N

© Crown Copyright (84114M)

Half-mile

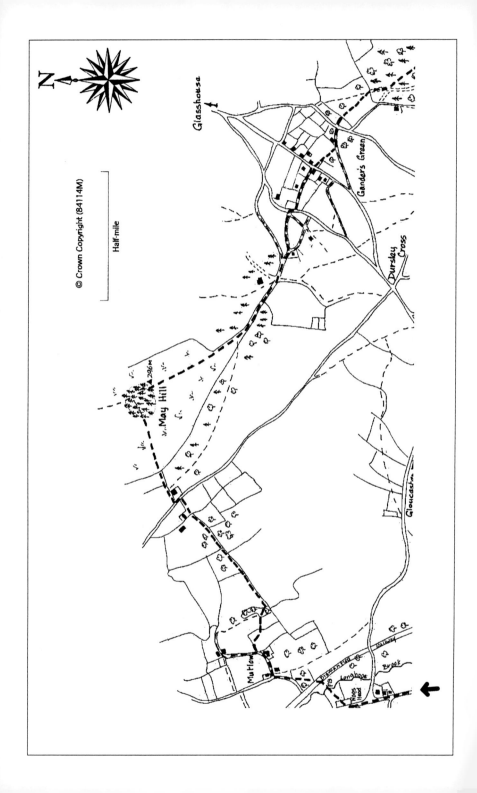

May Hill to Gloucester

From May Hill summit cross the plateau to the south-east and then descend through gates and an enclosed track through woodland. After a pole barrier continue down to a crossroad, and continue straight over into a lane shaded by an ancient hedgeline of oak, beech, sycamore and holly. At a fork in the path, keep right, and at the next, left, to reach a lane. To the left is the village of Glasshouse which has a pub and post office. Cross the lane slightly to the right, and continue downhill past cottages. Cross the next lane, over a stile into a field and descend to a further stile. *The chimney off to the right is the site of an old sawmill once driven by steam power.*

The stile gives access to an old track passing a cottage and picturesque pond on the left before crossing yet another lane. Off to the right is quaintly named Ganders Green. After a short enclosed path, walk up a field to the woodland of Brights Hill. Follow the forest track uphill until joining another track from the right which continues up the hill. The Gloucestershire Way turns left at this point, firstly along the contour and then gently downhill under a canopy of sweet chestnut, tall Scots pine, yew and the occasional oak, to arrive at the village school and parish church of Huntley.

The Huntley Yew, found behind the church, is said to be 1500 years old and certainly has an aura of extreme antiquity. The majestic Wellingtonia

Sequoias, native Californian Redwoods, are believed to indicate the line of the old carriage road to Gloucester.

Follow the school road down to cross the Gloucester - Ross road to a footpath. Walk down the left side of the field and cross stiles over the farm track and continue down to a gate. *The Severn Vale, the next feature of The Gloucestershire Way, provides the landscape ahead.*

Cross a road to a footpath a few paces to the right and walk down a long field towards woodland. About half way down the length of this field turn left over a footbridge, with the aptly named Round Hill directly ahead. By a quirk of the local footpath network the public right of way continues across this field towards the village of Huntley, but at the next boundary do not leave the field. Instead turn right over a stile in the fence, and cross diagonally towards a gate in the bottom hedge and a junction of paths. The alternative route from Longhope, which avoided May Hill, rejoins from the right.

The Gloucestershire Way turns left to follow an old hedge containing oak, elm, sycamore, ash and hawthorn and several other varieties along the base of Round Hill. Follow this pleasant route with views over the vale to the Cotswold scarp, to join a quiet country lane. Where this bends to the right, continue straight along Whitlow Lane. Approaching Whitlow Farm house the path turns left through a gate. Ignore a second gate straight ahead with a footpath to Birdwood Coppice, instead turn right, keeping the hedgerow on your left, and pass through a field gate next to a small brick building.

The fields beyond slope gently up to the village of Birdwood. This higher ground gives widening views across the Severn plain towards the 'high blue hills of Cotswold'. At the village, cross directly over the road and enter a green lane. Where this joins another road turn right after a few paces, through a field gate. Walking down this field, a line of three or four perry trees on the right indicate an old cider orchard. Indentations of the trunks show where they were protected by metal palings against browsing livestock. An indication of the importance of cider a generation or so ago. Minsterworth, on the banks of the Severn, was well known for its cider apple and perry orchards.

Six thousand apple varieties once grew in Britain and all are recorded in the National Apple Register. Almost half of these are still available from the National Fruit Trials Centre in Kent, the world's most comprehensive apple collection. The demise of apple varieties is attributed to the minimal choice provided by the retail trade. However, the large supermarket chains claim to supply what the customer demands, that is, apples of uniform size, appearance and taste. This has resulted in the widespread loss of old orchards.

In 1957 there were 64,000 acres of dessert apple in England, sadly reduced to 25,000 acres by 1990. Cider orchards too have greatly diminished, and many of the cider and perry orchards, which once enhanced many of the farms in Gloucestershire, are now gone. The commercial cider producers mostly grow their own limited varieties to maintain a standard produce. Fifty years ago the hundreds of varieties that grew throughout Britain exhibited a range of flavours that few people today have ever experienced. From the sharp and refreshing Beauty of Bath, in August, to D'Arcy Spice, that lived up to its name in spring, they provided a range of flavours that no other fruit could match.

'Coccagee and Bloody Butcher:
Slack-ma-Girdle,
Red Soldier and Lady's Finger,
Kingston Black, Bloody Turk,
Foxwhelp, Pawson, Tom Putt,
Bitter Sweet and Fatty Mutt.'

At the bottom of the field pass through a gate and cross the next field to a gate onto a footbridge. Angle to the left up the higher ground in front and then walk down to cross a farm bridge. Turn left through a gate and keep to the right hand hedge of a long meadow. Around a corner pass a cattle trough and turn right through a narrow gate.

Alternative route:
The Gloucestershire Way crosses the railway in about half a mile. To cross by a road level crossing, turn right through a further gate and follow the left edge of the field to reach Leycourt Farm. Turn left on the road and shortly after the level crossing, rejoin The Gloucestershire Way outside Green Farm.

Turn left, again keeping to the right hand hedgerow of a long field to a gate in the furthest corner. Follow the next hedgerow as it curves round to reach the main Gloucester -Cardiff railway line. Cross the tracks with great care. *Although there is good visibility in either direction, remember that InterCity reaches speeds in excess of 100 mph.* Walk to the farm buildings to reach the road, where the alternative route rejoins.

Turn left and follow the road bending to the right. After 100 yards ignore an inset gateway on the left and turn left through the next gate immediately after. Walk down the field, passing close to the angle of a hedge on the left, and then incline right to find a footbridge in the next hedge. Cross the next field on the same line towards a lone ash tree, keeping the higher ground of Denny Hill on the right to a second footbridge. Continue on the same line across the remnants of an old cider orchard to reach a lane called Oakle Street.

from Cider-House

Only a few remember the cider days,
the shuffle of clogged feet on the littered floor;
fruit piled high in the round baskets,

MAY HILL TO GLOUCESTER

trundled in from the warm harvesting,
the nodding horses waiting patiently by the orchard gate,
waggons bumping along the ruts to the cool house.
And then all day the golden liquid
trickling, bubble and drop, through the creaking wood,
the engine still humming the same, soft song,
pipes, hogsheads, and puncheons filled to the bung,
the raw juice heady, overflowing,
mashed straw and pulp thrown to the pigs.

They are gone now, cider-house and orchards,
the billowing tides of blossoms riding the slopes,
with early bees raiding, and Severn, a silver eel,
twisting to the sea on the far-away skyline.

The magical names remain,
those old apples of cidered Gloucestershire,
Skyrmes Kernel, Dymock Red, and Forest Styre,
Black Foxwhelps and Redstreak; such honeyed sounds,
pure English poetry in my country ears.
I say each one to myself now, lovely on my tongue,
as ripe and rounded as cider itself;
drunk with long memories from a china mug,
the fire glowing on a winter evening.
Leonard Clark

Follow the lane to the right for 40 yards to a brick built entrance splay
on the left, and take the footpath alongside leading into another orchard.
Pass the corner of a cottage garden to reach the Gloucester - Chepstow
road. Turn left, for a hundred yards and cross to a kissing gate and join
the Severn Way, a footpath along the floodbank of the Severn, to reach
Minsterworth church.

The Severn Way is a proposed long-distance footpath, on both sides of the river from the source to the sea. Sections of the west bank are open and signposted but the only designated length of path in Gloucestershire to date is on the east bank.

F.W. (Will) Harvey was born at Hartpury but spent much of his early life at Minsterwoth. Before their service in the First World War, Will Harvey met Ivor Gurney, who had been a fellow pupil at King's School, Gloucester and they associated closely in their appreciation of music, poetry and the countryside. Both are recognised as fine poets who have written evocative scenes of Gloucestershire. Will Harvey is buried in the churchyard and his early home, Redlands, is nearby (see Appendix 2).

Spring came by water to Broadoak this year.
I saw her clear
Though on the earth a sprinkling
Of snowdrops shone, the unwrinkling
Bright curve of Severn River
was of her gospel first giver.
F W Harvey

* * *

Strong Severn all aglow,
But tideless, running slow:
Far Cotswolds all a shimmer,
Blue Bredon leagues away
Huge Malverns, farther; dimmer....
Ivor Gurney

Alternative route:
From the church, Church Lane can be followed through Minsterworth passing Calcott's Green to reach High Cross Farm at the edge of the village.

The Gloucestershire Way continues with the Severn Way along the river bank and can be followed all the way to Gloucester: There are fine views here over the water meadows to the Cathedral. The Gloucestershire Way leaves the river just before reaching the power lines which cross the river. After a stile on the riverbank, follow the path curving inland to a sluice. Do not cross but follow the path left, around a low-lying field to a stile. Turn right over this and walk up fields to a further stile, close to a cottage. At the lane cross to a stile and walk across the field to a road junction.

Take the stile on the right and cross two more stiles, then pass close to a hedge corner to a stile and gate at the road. Cross the stile and immediately turn right over a further stile alongside a driveway, then skirt to the left of a pond in a landscaped garden. Go through a small gate in a fence to a stile in the thick hedgerow. Over this, turn left and cross two further stiles in quick succession. Walk down the next field, passing under a large oak tree. Cross a farm track to a stile in the hedge.

Continue on the same line down the next field, slightly to the right of the concrete electricity poles, to cross another farm track. Pass to the right of the last concrete pole to a stile at the bottom of a slight slope. Cross the farmyard beyond to a stile and gate next to a timber electricity pole. Cross the next field, to the left of the farm buildings and cross the farm track by gates opposite each other. Follow the hedge to a footbridge and then the same line across the next field, to reach the headland and a gate onto a farm road.

47

Alternative route:
Although there is no alternative to crossing the railway, at the time of writing a diversion is under consideration which would allow walkers to cross the tracks by the adjacent farm access road. This is well provided with warning signs, a telephone and level surface, and is therefore more convenient than the existing right of way.

Cross the road and follow a path around an attractive reservoir, often teeming with bird life. The footpath continues along the headland for about 100 yards to a stile in the railway boundary fence. Cross the railway with extreme care as high speed trains approach almost silently. At the further stile turn right along the farm track, the bed of old railway sidings, and turn left at another farm access road across the railway.

Follow the farm track to the verge alongside the Gloucester-Ross road and turn right towards Over. This will usually be a noisy and uncomfortable few minutes, but shortly after passing the Dog Inn, on the opposite side of the road, turn right to old Over Bridge, an English Heritage site. This is pleasantly isolated from the roar of the traffic and provides the start of a quiet route into the city.

Designed by Thomas Telford and copied from a bridge over the Seine itwas opened in 1831. The arch is a graceful ellipse enhanced by the chamfering of the stonework of the arch to ease the flow of floodwaters. A keen eye will detect where the crown of the arch sank 10 inches when the scaffolding was first removed in 1831. No doubt a heart-stopping moment for the engineer, although Telford is said to have anticipated this! Telford's bridge replaced a 13th Century structure of eight arches.

Alternative route:
During the winter months the River Severn is liable to overflow causing flooding or waterlogging of the low-lying areas between the two channels of the river. The only option then is to continue along the road from the Dog Inn into Gloucester. For most of the year, however, several routes are available without using roads. A slightly longer route from the bridge detours to the right under the railway arch, and follows both arms of the Severn, around the wide expanse of the Port Ham and Oxleaze, to reach a car parking area with a footbridge leading directly into the heart of Gloucester docks and the City.

At the time of writing there is a proposal for a new cycle and walkway between Over and Gloucester.

Modern roadworks have removed much of the old causeway between Telford's bridge and the city, and a direct route no longer exists for The Gloucestershire Way. From the bridge walk down the slope to a footbridge and turn right passing under the viaduct, alongside the railway. *The Cathedral tower, framed by the bridge piers, creates a powerful image of ancient and modern.* Emerge onto a sports field, Gloucester Irish Association hurling pitch, and follow the right hand boundary to the brick railway viaduct.

Pass underneath to a gate and follow a track through young woodland to the dual carriageway. Turn left along the footway and use the underpass and footbridge to cross the east channel of the River Severn at Westgate Bridge. The Gloucestershire Way continues northwards along the east bank of the river, although many walkers will wish to visit Gloucester's historic cathedral and docks.

The Vale of Severn extends for more than 30 miles along the estuary, bounded by the Cotswold scarp to the east and the high ground of Dean to the west. To the north Tewkesbury stands at the gateway to the

Worcestershire plain and the Vale of Evesham. Viewed from nearby Bredon Hill, Gloucester and the Cathedral stand boldly in the centre of the Vale. To the south the ever widening estuary dominates the vale.

Until the building of the Severn Bridge near Chepstow, Gloucester was for centuries, the major crossing point of the Severn and an ancient frontier and centre for trade. The Romans early established a fort there and Glevum later became a place of retirement for Roman officers and administrators. Wherever a hole is dug in the City it is said that some 2000 years of occupation will be found.

Following the Romans and Saxons, the Normans commenced work on the Cathedral. The tower, 225 feet high, remains a landmark for many miles around, clearly seen from most points on Cotswold and as far away as Bredon and the Malvern Hills. In 1089 William the Conqueror gave instructions for the preparation of the Domesday Book from his Parliament in Gloucester.

Edward II, murdered at nearby Berkeley, is entombed in the Cathedral which, as a result, became a mecca for pilgrims. The resulting prosperity gave the City's population of 3000 inhabitants a total of five monasteries and twelve churches which later gave rise to Shakespeare's comment 'as sure as God's in Gloucester'. Unfortunately, the City's elders backed Cromwell in the Civil War withstanding a determined and expensive siege by the King's army in 1643. On his restoration the King sought his dues and caused the City walls, which would have been the equal of York or Chester today, to be demolished.

Gloucester was granted a Charter as a port by Elizabeth I in 1580 complete with its own Customs House. However, Bristol mounted such a furious lobby that the Charter was revoked within two years and it was not until the completion of the Gloucester - Sharpness Canal, three centuries later, that Gloucester again became a port. Gloucester Docks have now been restored and together with several old sailing vessels usually moored there, maintain the link with the City's trading history. Although now a popular marina and tourist centre, commercial motor barges, of up to 400 tons, still ply the canal to Sharpness, and the river north to Tewkesbury and Worcester.

Opened in 1989 The Severn Way runs for 50 miles along the east bank of the Severn from Tewkesbury to Sheperdine just south of Berkeley. Following roads, footpaths and bridleways, often along the flood bank, the route passes through ancient communities and scenes. During the walk the river changes from tree-bordered tranquillity at Tewkesbury to a mile wide tidal estuary at Sheperdine. It is planned that the Severn Way will continue to Worcester and beyond and also for the creation of a contiuous path on the west bank.

The Glevum Way is a 22 mile long footpath circling the City.

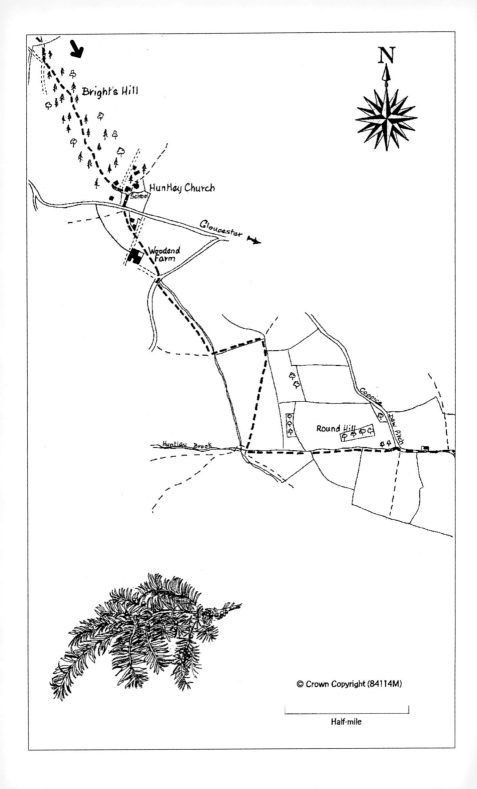

Bright's Hill

Huntley Church

School

Gloucester

Woodend Farm

Huntley Brook

Round Hill

Coppice

Dow Pitch

N

© Crown Copyright (84114M)

Half-mile

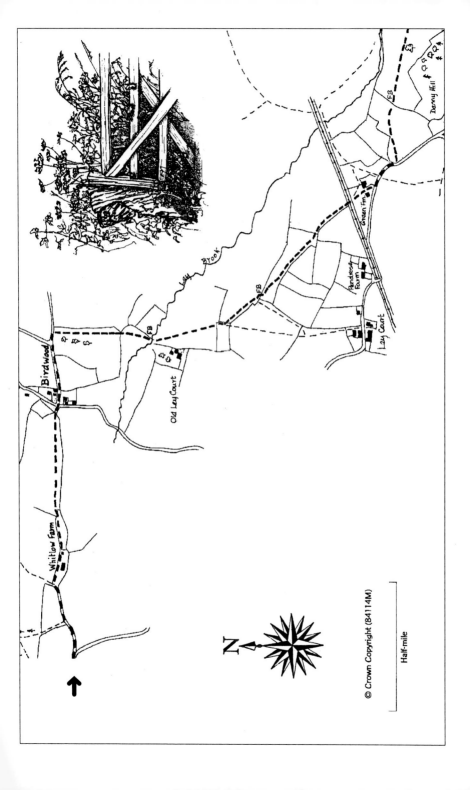

Birdwood

Whitlow Farm

Old Ley Court

Leddy Brook

FB

FB

Green Fm

Parchrose Farm

Ley Court

Denny Hill

FB

N

© Crown Copyright (84114M)

Half-mile

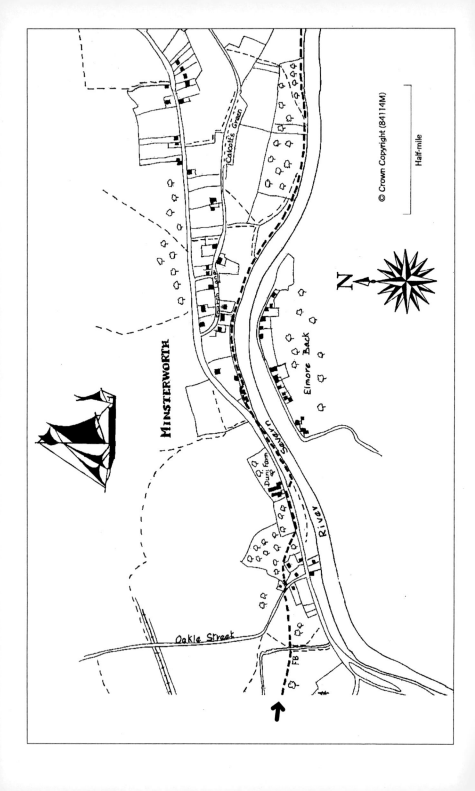

MINSTERWORTH

Calcotts Green

Elmore Back

Dunii Farm

River Severn

Oakle Street

FB

N

Half-mile

© Crown Copyright (84114M)

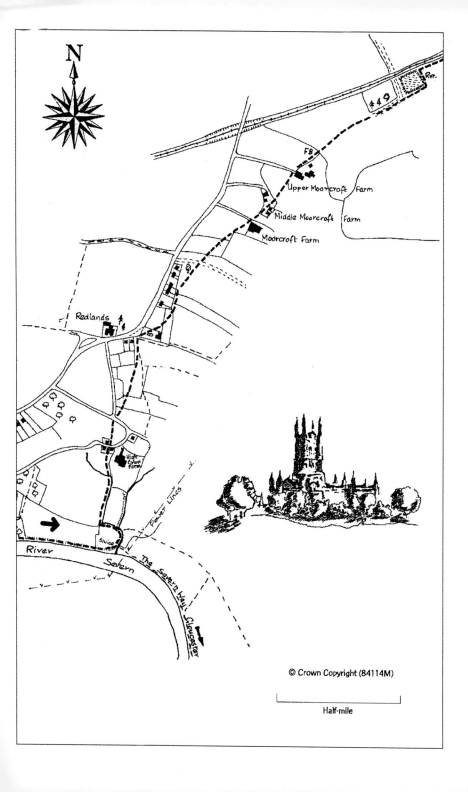

N

FB

Upper Moorcroft Farm

Middle Moorcroft Farm

Moorcroft Farm

Redlands

High Cross Farm

Power Lines

Sluice

River Severn

The Severn Way, Gloucester

© Crown Copyright (84114M)

Half-mile

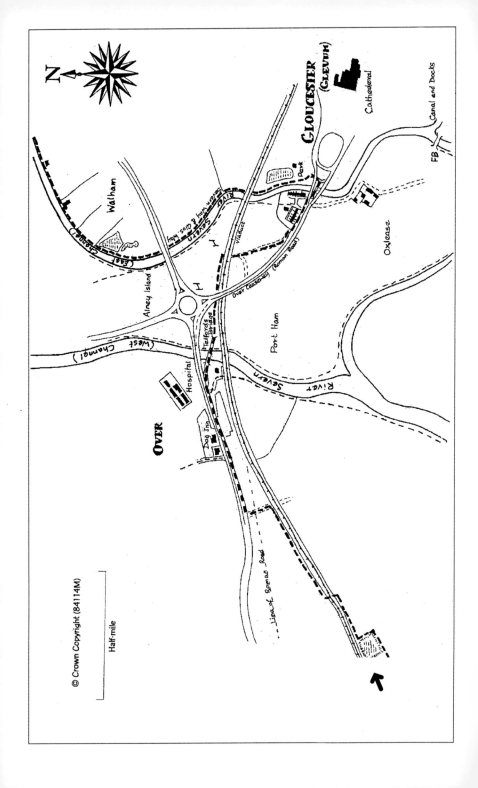

Gloucester to Crickley

From Westgate Bridge The Gloucestershire Way shares the east bank of the river with The Severn Way and the recently created Glevum Way, a 22 mile route which follows the City boundary. Leave the small park and lake near Westgate Bridge, passing under the railway viaduct. Continue for almost two miles to the Globe Inn and shortly afterwards turn right to the road where the riverside path is interrupted by a drainage channel.

The Gloucestershire Way now leaves the river to cross the vale towards the higher ground of Cotswold. Turn left along the road passing an old manor house, Abloads Court. At the road junction fork right and after 300 yards turn right onto a footpath. Follow this to a stile and then cross the long field beyond, to the corner of an orchard and continue to a stile under a willow tree. The path from the stile is sometimes difficult to follow through crops as the bridge over the Broadboard Brook is out of sight down the contour. Pass under the power lines, keeping the nearest pylon well to your left, on a line towards Chosen Hill standing out against the backdrop of the Cotswold scarp. At the bridge continue straight on to the Horsebere Brook and follow this to reach the Gloucester - Tewkesbury Road at Longford Bridge.

Cross the road and from the stile ignore a footpath continuing alongside the Horsebere, and instead cross the field diagonally to Hatherley Brook, which is followed for over a mile to Frog Furlong Lane. At the lane a stile and signpost can be found to the left of the gate, which is often padlocked. Cross the road and continue following Hatherley Brook along the edge of a golf course. A surprisingly attractive route exists for the next mile through a green corridor between the urban edges of Gloucester and Cheltenham.

Where Hatherley Brook forks follow the right hand stream, now Norman's Brook. The path changes from the right bank to the left at a brick built bridge. Follow this bank to the Gloucester - Cheltenham road at Half Way Bridge. Cross the road and continue alongside Norman's Brook passing the boundary to Staverton airfield.

An old wartime pill box, complete with machine gun embrasures, above the path, is a relic of the airfield's Second World War defences. Staverton, together with nearby Brockworth and Moreton Valence airfields, played a prominent role in Britain's air defences during that period. The Whittle Jet engine and the Gloster Meteor aircraft were later developed at Brockworth.

Approaching the dual carriageway between Cheltenham and Gloucester, the path contours to the left and follows the embankment for about 100 yards to an underpass. The public footpath turns right, again following the embankment, before branching left to follow Norman's Brook to a gate at a farm drive. Cross and continue along the brook and pass close to a timber electricity pole to a stile in the fence immediately beyond. A few yards further on the path forks right over a stile to a subway under the railway. Follow the next meadow, midway between the motorway and the stream on the right, now the Ham Brook. Cross the stream by the farm access near a large oak tree and walk up to the road.

Turn left over the motorway and take the footpath immediately on the right, which follows the edge of the motorway to a stile. Continue for about 50 yards and turn left over a further stile, cross the field diagonally to the far right hand corner where the stile is sometimes obscured by thick hedge growth. Continue along the next paddock between willow and ash trees and cross two stiles in succession. After the second, turn right over a footbridge and walk up the field beyond towards Badgeworth Church. Cross the lane and incline right into an enclosed path which leads into the churchyard and walk through to the lych gate at the entrance.

From the church gate cross the village green, where a signpost indicates a footpath to the right, 'Brockworth and Bentham 2 miles'. The Gloucestershire Way follows the metalled track straight on and where this bends to the right continue down to a gate. Walk up the field beyond to the edge of the trees on the left. Continue towards a gate in the next hedge but at the last moment drop down left to a footbridge. Cross this and follow the path alongside the brook over several stiles. Where the brook bends to the right, cross directly over the next short field and join a pleasant enclosed green track. After 100 yards, turn right over a footbridge and continue for a short distance before turning left at a hedge end. Walk up the next field past a tree and join a track which leads to the Cheltenham - Stroud road.

Turn left for a short distance and turn into a lane on the right passing Dawn Nurseries. Follow the twists and turns for about a quarter of a mile to a sharp right bend. Ignore the footpath through a gateway to the left, and walk straight ahead up a drive. After the drive bends to the right the footpath turns right immediately before a cottage. Turn left at the end of the cottage garden and cross a narrow paddock to a stile and continue over fields and further stiles to reach Green Field Farm.

Join the farm lane and follow this to the right, past the farmhouse, and at the end of the stable block, turn left to a bridle gate. Immediately turn right through a field gate and follow the line of a watercourse uphill and, after about 150 yards, turn right to a stile over a further watercourse. Walk uphill to a stone slab stile on the skyline and continue on the same line up the steepening contours over rough, tussocky grass.

The line of the path can be followed past timber electricity poles. At the second pole turn right through a gate and continue uphill, with a house and garden off to the left, to reach a stone slab stile at the road. Within a few paces a choice of paths climb steeply up to the Devil's Table.

East Wind
Cool air moves there up on Cotswold edge,
By Crickley's bastion or the Shurdington wedge,
Grey grass rustles, the harebells dance and the east
Wind has no good influences on the cattle at feast.

Naked land-slides show, away down hill mist-shades cover
The land where South-West once moved high like a lover,
With colour and boy's glory and breath of renewal:
There also, that valley, for this dry air is a fuel.

But the great steeps keep one in right hoping still,
Mighty the upstanding curving of the golden-crowned hill
Crickley, where scabious and serious thistle nods,
And there is good hiding place for the old gods.
Ivor Gurney

Immediately above the Devil's Table, keep the boundary fence to the right and climb up to the plateau of Crickley Hill Iron Age fort. *The excavations and the Country Park, jointly owned by Gloucestershire County Council and the National Trust, can be explored and there is an Information Centre.*

The landscape we walk through in Gloucestershire today is fairly modern and 200 years ago or so the countryside was much wilder and overgrown. The lines of communication were the ancient trackways through the countryside but particularly on the high ground either side of the Severn. First used for movement and migration, the trackways evolved for the transportation of goods and livestock and to connect the habitations and villages that arose, particularly in Anglo-Saxon times. The lines of these old trackways are still largely used today and can be traced clearly on Ordnance Survey maps. Tarmac has overtaken many but other green ways, hidden lanes and tracks still exist.

The Cotswold Ridgeway is part of the Jurassic Way, which traversed England from the Humber to the Somerset Avon. The route, winding to avoid river bottoms and marshy ground, traverses the Cotswold edge, connecting hill forts, tumuli and earthworks throughout its length. The main route of the Cotswold Ridgeway crosses The Gloucestershire Way near Crickley and again near Farmcote above Winchcombe. A subsidiary route closely follows The Gloucestershire Way between Foxcote and Stow-on-the-Wold but is now predominantly tarmacadam.

The Gloucestershire Way now joins the Cotswold Way National Trail on a permissive path. Ignore the Cotswold Way waymarks pointing left and continue straight on alongside the boundary wall. After a kissing gate in a fence, cross the outer mound of the hill fort. The Cotswold Way follows the wall but a well used route slightly uphill to the left may be preferred. This passes through attractive open beech wood intermixed with holly and oak. Where this track bends left, and starts to climb, fork right through a bridlegate and rejoin the Cotswold Way. Close to the boundary fence to a cricket field, turn right through a gate on to the busy roundabout adjacent to the Air Balloon Inn.

Currently being assessed as a National Trail, the Cotswold Way follows the Cotswold escarpment for 100 miles, from Chipping Campden in the north to Bath away to the south. The Cotswold Way links with the Heart of England Way and with the proposed Three Rivers Way.

Refreshments are usually available throughout the day at the Air Balloon and the landlord may be amenable to cars being left by customers starting circular walks from the pub. Alternatively, there is public car parking at Barrow Wake viewpoint, accessible from the Cirencester Road about a mile uphill.

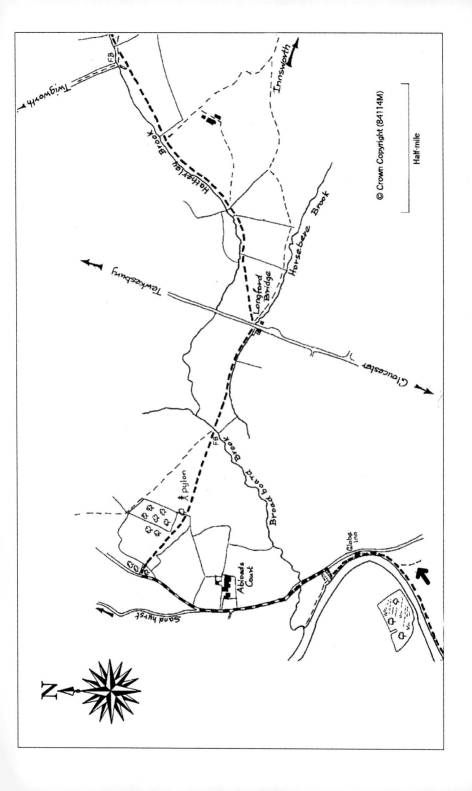

N

Twigworth

FB

Innsworth

Hatherley Brook

Tewkesbury

Longford Bridge

Horsebere Brook

Gloucester

© Crown Copyright (84114M)

Half-mile

FB

Broad Brook

Pylon

Sandhurst

Abloads Court

Globe Inn

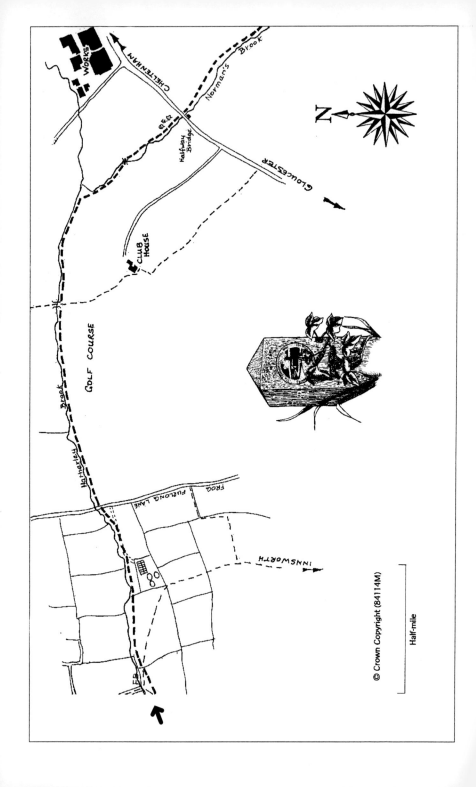

© Crown Copyright (84114M)

Half-mile

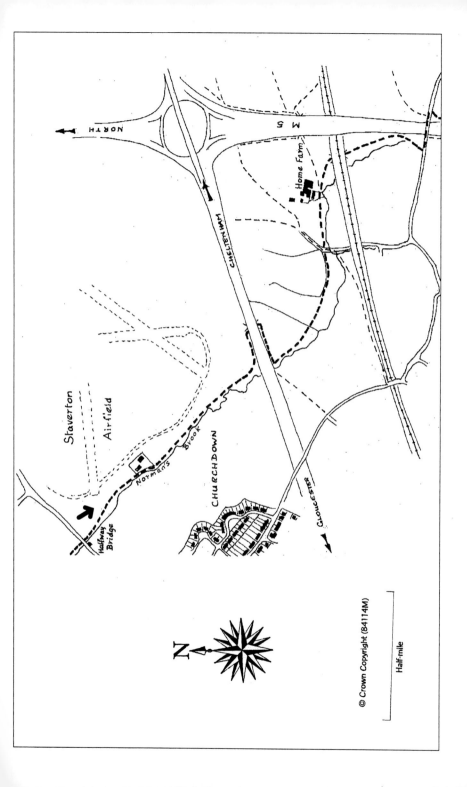

NORTH

M 5

Home Farm

CHELTENHAM

Staverton

Airfield

Brook

Normans

CHURCHDOWN

GLOUCESTER

Halfway
Bridge

N

© Crown Copyright (84114M)

Half-mile

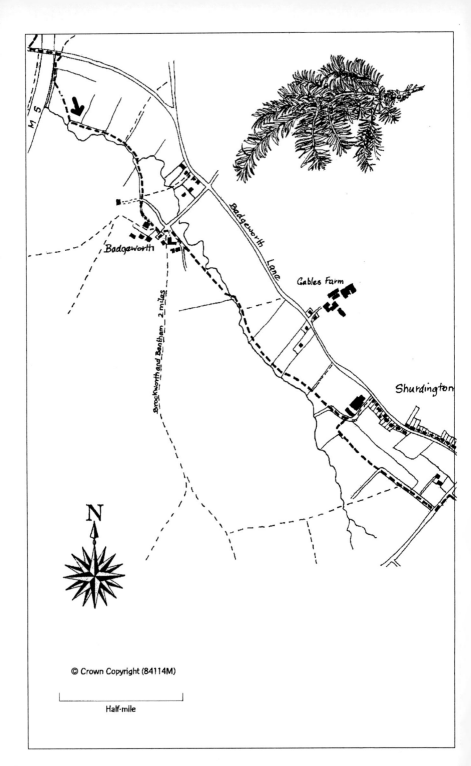

M 5

Badgeworth Lane

Badgeworth

Brockworth and Bentham 2 miles

Gables Farm

Shurdington

N

© Crown Copyright (84114M)

Half-mile

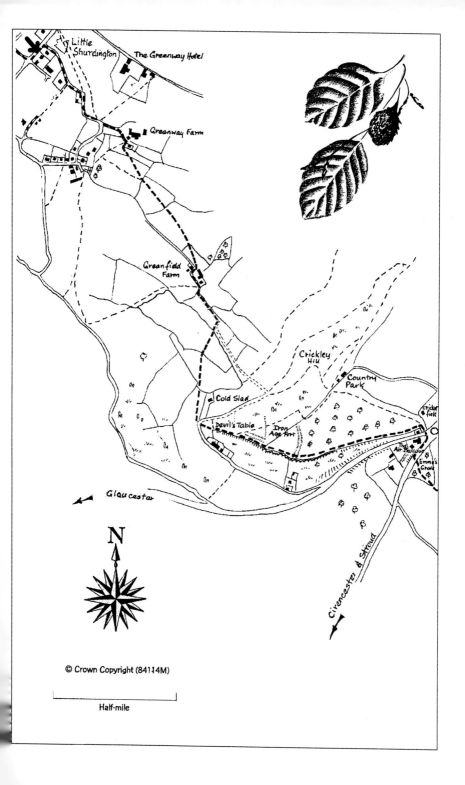

Little
Shurdington
The Greenway Hotel

Greenway Farm

Greenfield
Farm

Crickley
Hill

Cold Slad

Country
Park

Devil's Table

Iron
Age Fort

Crickley
field

The
Air Balloon

Emma's
Grove

Gloucester

Cirencester & Stroud

N

Half-mile

Crickley to Salperton

Slightly uphill from the Air Balloon, cross the road to a footpath, signposted Cowley, into the woodland at Emma's Grove where the path curves uphill and leaves the wood through a gap. Walk straight up the next field, cross a farm track over stiles and continue up to a hedge. Follow the left hand side to a lane and cross this into Rushwood Kennels, usually a short but noisy interlude. From the kennels the path follows the wall through a short enclosed path and then descends an attractive valley through newly planted woodland where a single mature tree gives the line of the parish boundary.

Up There
On Cotswold edge there is a field and that
Grows thick with corn and speedwell and the mat
Of thistles, of the tall kind; Rome lived there,
Some hurt centurion got his grant or tenure,
Built farm with fowls and pigsties and wood-piles,
Waited for service custom between whiles.
The farmer ploughs up coins in the wet-earth-time,
He sees them on the topple of crests gleam,
Or run down furrow; and halts and does let them lie
Like a small black island in brown immensity,
Till his wonder is ceased, and his great hand picks up the penny.
Red pottery easy discovered, no searching needed...

68

CRICKLEY TO SALPERTON

One wonders what farms were like, no searching needed,
As now the single kite hovering still
By the coppice there, level with the flat of the hill.
Ivor Gurney

At Coldwell Bottom, turn left climbing a little and then follow an old road contouring the hillside. This is joined after half a mile by a track from the left before dropping down to a junction. Coberley village can be visited by taking the lane to the left. Preferably, a short distance further on, where the lane bends right, continue on a rough track which curves left to the village.

Alternative route:
To avoid the village altogether, where the rough track curves left, keep straight on down on a field edge track, an ancient road, to Coberley Mill. Cross the River Churn and walk up to the Cheltenham-Cirencester road.

During the traverse of Cotswold The Gloucestershire Way crosses five of the many Cotswold streams. The Churn, Coln, Windrush and Dikler all rise near the watershed where the ancient Cotswold Ridgeway ran, and flow east and south to the Thames. The fifth and last stream is the Isbourne which also rises on the watershed, near Charlton Abbots, but follows the winding valleys down to Winchcombe and thence north to join Shakespeare's Avon flowing into the Severn at Tewkesbury.

Coberley still has, for the time being, a post office with limited opening hours. The parish church is interesting, being approached through the arched gateway to Coberley Court, where the church is an integral part of the medieval design.

Alternative route:
From the road outside the church walk steeply up to the main Cheltenham - Cirencester road. A few yards to the left, cross to a footpath which climbs to Upper Coberley.

Just past the arched entrance to the church, turn right through a gate adjacent to a cottage and follow the footpath past ponds to an open field. Then incline left to reach the road close to the lane coming up from Coberley Mill.

The now vanished Hall at Coberley was another home of the Berkeleys of South Gloucestershire. Sir William Whittington, father of Dick, married the widow of Sir Thomas Berkeley without the Royal licence (selling rich widows was a lucrative perquisite of the Crown). Sir William was outlawed until he paid a heavy fine for his presumption. Dick lived at Coberley until he sought fame as 'thrice Lord Mayor of London'.

Cross the road with care, the traffic is very fast, to join a bridleway to Upper Coberley. Walk through the village to a T-junction and turn left for 150 yards to a footpath and bridleway a few yards apart on the right. Both routes go to Needlehole.

The footpath passes an electricity pylon and takes a line uphill slightly to the right of the power lines. On reaching the woodland the path follows the edge to join the bridleway at Needlehole. *This is the site of yet another ancient abandoned village.* After half a mile this pleasant stone track joins a narrow ancient lane which is followed uphill to a junction, with a track on the right to Foxcote Hill Farm and a bridleway to the left. Continue up the lane between walls surmounted by ash, hawthorn, blackthorn and wild rose for about 220 yards to a crossover of paths.

The Gloucestershire Way takes the path on the right, descending steeply with wide views over Foxcote to Shipton Oliffe and Shipton Solers in front, and Sevenhampton and Brockhampton to the left. Drop down to a gate on to the bridleway track and follow this to the left between an avenue of limes and maples which will be a glorious sight and smell for years to come.

Alternative route:
Continue along the bridleway enjoying the fine avenue of trees, now a mixture of rowan and maple. At a lane, either turn right and rejoin the main route through Foxcote, or continue across, on the bridleway, before turning right at farm buildings to rejoin The Gloucestershire Way.

After 200 yards a footpath on the right forks diagonally down to a recently planted area of woodland. Cross this through a pedestrian gate to a stile. Follow the edge of mature woodland to another stile, and down through a field gate to pass alongside a horse schooling area and through the stable yard to the road in Foxcote village.

Turn right for a few paces and then left into a cul de sac until a gate gives access into a field. Follow the boundary of the next two fields to cross a road. On the other side the footpath has been diverted from the right hand side of the hedgerow to the left, around a golf course. Follow this headland path down to join an old green lane, now the golf course entrance.

Turn left for a few paces and follow the old road, signposted as a bridleway, to the right crossing the infant Coln, which rises near Andoversford, behind the Frogmill Inn.

Samuel Rudder in his History of Gloucestershire (1779) described 'a good inn called Frogmill on the east bank of the Colne'.

The Frogmill was the first staging post of the 'Glocester Flying Machine' the famous Gloucester to Oxford mail coach. The 105 mile journey between Gloucester and London was completed in two days, was then the equivalent of flying.

Continue up to cross the Cheltenham - Oxford road. From the corner opposite, take the footpath through a kissing gate, across a driveway to a second gate and walk down the sheep pasture to a further kissing gate and stream. Cross the drive to an attractive house beneath two enormous sycamore trees. Walk up the short grass slope on the other side to join the village street into Shipton Oliffe. Pass a chapel on the left and glimpse a ford down a lane to the right and continue along the street, with views of the manor house to the right. After passing the church ignore the next turning to the left but take the next fork left, uphill to a crossroads.

The Gloucestershire Way continues straight ahead signposted 'No Through Road'. After 270 yards, as the track bends left and starts to climb past North Farm House, turn right, at a notice 'North Farm and Shipton Downs', and pass between the barns. Follow this track past a cottage and fork left at an electricity pylon to reach the road. Cross over and walk down to the secluded hamlet of Hampen.

Alternative route:
The road bears left past the manor and climbs uphill to Hampen House.

Where the road bends sharply left, a footpath forks right through the farm buildings. At the last barn pass through a gate on the right and drop down left to cross a stream then up to a stile at the road. Immediately after the left hand bend turn right into another old road and follow this, over a crossroad, to Salperton.

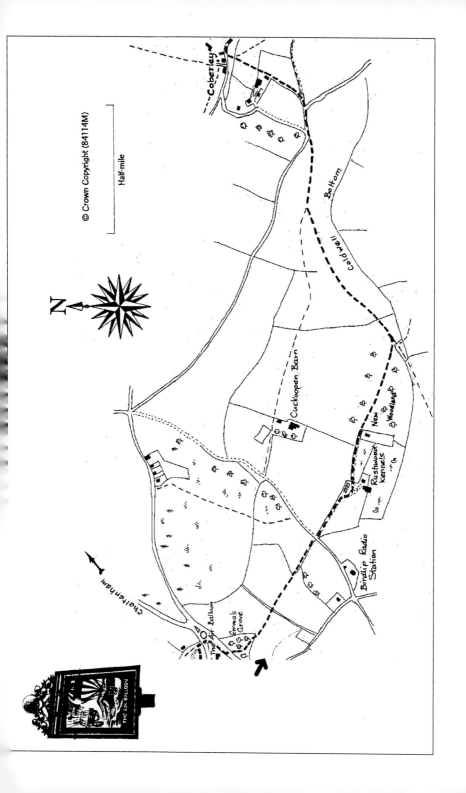

© Crown Copyright (84114M)

Half-mile

N

THE AIR BALLOON

Coberley

Coldwell Bottom

Cuckoopen Barn

New Woodland

Rushwood Kennels

Birdlip Radio Station

Cheltenham

The Air Balloon

Emma's Grove

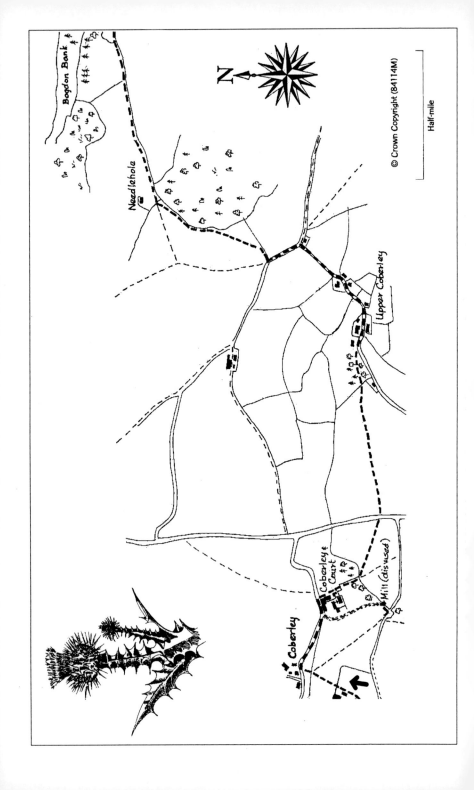

N

© Crown Copyright (84114M)

Half-mile

Bogdon Bank

Needlehole

Upper Coberley

Coberley

Coberley Court

Mill (disused)

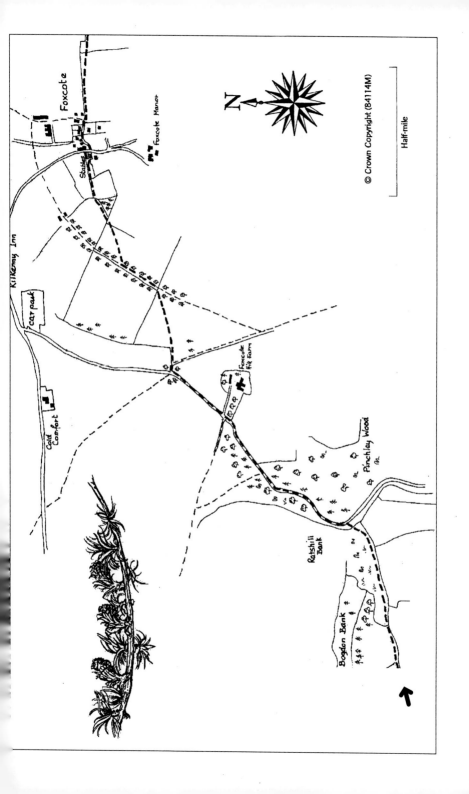

Foxcote

Foxcote Manor

Stables

Kilkenny Inn

car park

Cold Comfort

Foxcote Hit Farm

Pinchlay Wood

Ratshill Bank

Bogdan Bank

N

© Crown Copyright (84114M)

Half-mile

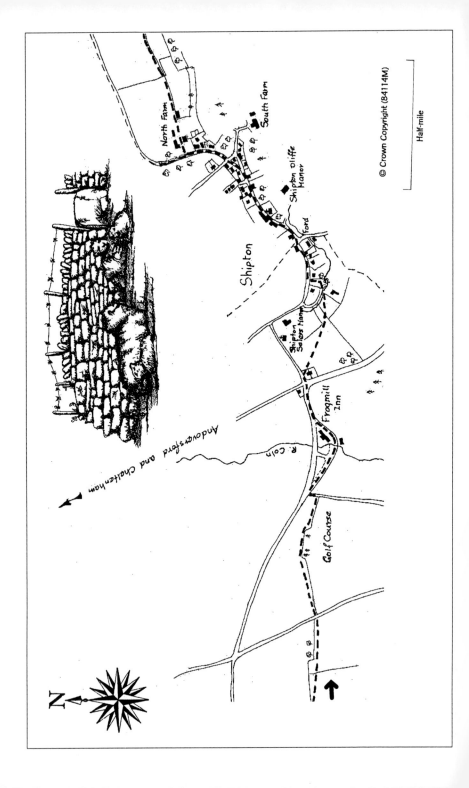

North Farm

South Farm

Shipton oliffe Manor

Ford

Shipton

Shipton Solers Manor

Frogmill Inn

R. Coln

Golf Course

Andoversford and Cheltenham

N

© Crown Copyright (84114M)

Half-mile

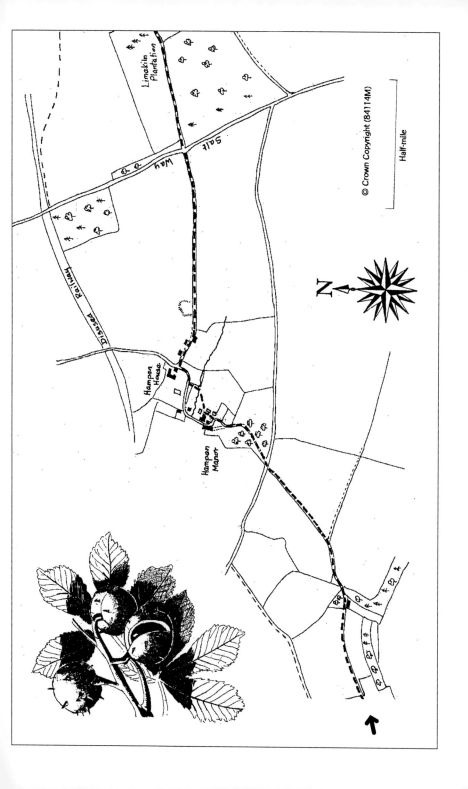

Limekiln Plantation

Salt Way

Disused Railway

Hampen House

Hampen Manor

N

© Crown Copyright (84114M)

Half-mile

Salperton to Stow-on-the-Wold

When Cotswold was still open country, salt ways followed prehistoric tracks. Deviations of these connected many of the manors owning salt rights at Droitwich.

Salperton, or a village on the saltway, mentioned in the Domesday Book, remains a feudal village largely owned by a Lord of the Manor.

Approaching Salperton, The Gloucestershire Way turns right, uphill, at the War Memorial. Past the entrance to Salperton Park and church, the old road then follows along a glorious ridgeway to Farhill Farm. After the farm the surfaced track ends and a bridleway curves down the contours to follow the valley bottom to the right to join a cross bridleway. Turn left uphill to Kites Hill Barn where the track joins the road. Turn left and almost immediately right into a tree-lined road into Notgrove.

At a junction follow the road straight on between stone pillars signed to 'Manor Farm, Glebe Farm and Church'. This narrows between a wall and a barn, to a terrace with an open view onto a valley landscaped with imposing trees.

Cotswold Tiles

The finest roofs in all the land are made from Cotswold stone,
And the mason gives each tile a name like children of his own.
By length and breadth the tally runs, by width and depth and size,
And the mason knows them all by name, for he is very wise.
Long Day, Short Day, Moreday and Muffity,
Lye-byes and Bottomers, each a name receives:
Wivett, Beck, and Cussomes, Cutting, Third and Bachelor,
Smallest under roof-ridge, largest over eaves.

Each tile in its own special place is hung with loving care,
And they weather down the ages in the mellow Cotswold air:
Twenty-six in all there are – the family's not small,
I can but tell you one or two, I can't remember all.

Long Day, Short Day, Moreday and Muffity,
Lye-byes and Bottomers, each a name receives.
Wivett, Beck and Cussomes, Cutting, Third and Bachelor,
Smallest under roof-ridge, largest over eaves.

Edward Berryman

Descend through the field gate and climb the slope to a further gate on the right at the top. Turn right onto a track, and then left into a fine avenue of beeches. On leaving the avenue turn right on the road and walk through Cold Aston to the Plough Inn, ideally located for further refreshment.

Aston Blank, or Cold Aston as the locals prefer to call it, is windswept and bleak at times. The Enclosures in the 1750s gave us this landscape. Where we may see a few hundred sheep now thousands were previously grazed on the vast commons and sheep walks, providing the wealth which built the great churches at Northleach and Stow-on-the-Wold.

The Gloucestershire Way continues past the pub and down the road to the left of the village green. Cross the stream in the valley bottom and continue up the road for about 400 yards to a coppice on the left. A footpath leaves the road and follows the edge of the coppice and field. Cross a track in the valley bottom slightly left to a gateway and follow the headland path up the slope to the left of the hedge.

On reaching a road cross over and again follow the headland path down to a lane leading to Little Aston Mill, now a private house. Cross the River Windrush and walk up close to a house to join a bridleway, and take the left fork. Shortly after the second boundary fence, turn right through a gate and cross the field diagonally to Buckle Street. Cross over and continue on a further bridleway.

Buckle Street (Buggildsway) follows, for the most part, much older tracks than its name suggests (named after Anglo-Saxon Lady Burghild AD 709). It is a lofty and lonely way with a definite feeling of ancient remoteness in parts.

At the next crossroads continue down into Lower Slaughter, *(Slohter now Slough – a wet miry place on a road, wet uneven ground).*

Alternative route:
Cross the footbridge over the River Eye, which rises a short distance to the north at Eyeford Park, to the old mill complete with its water wheel. Follow the village street around to the right to reach the church.

From the footbridge, turn right and follow the river to the church. Take the footpath on the right, which passes the corner of a house. Walk across pleasant meadows towards Stow-on-the-Wold sharing the path with the Heart of England Way for a short distance.

> *The Heart of England Way, 80 miles in length, links The Staffordshire Way at Cannock Chase with the Cotswold Way at Chipping Campden and has recently been extended for a further 20 miles to join the Oxfordshire Way at Bourton-on-the-Water*
>
> *Commencing at Bourton-on-the-Water in Gloucestershire The Oxfordshire Way soon leaves the County on its 65 mile journey eastwards to Henley on Thames. The path joins the Ridgeway on the Chilterns.*

After a quarter of a mile cross the unmarked line of ancient Ryknild Street, to be met again at Condicote. Continue for over a mile to a junction of paths and turn right to Hyde Mill.

Ryknild Street proceeded from Roman Bourton-on-the-Water, to Derby and York. The Gloucestershire Way again crosses Ryknild Street at Condicot where Condicot Lane follows the line of this ancient route.

Approaching Hyde Mill, cross a bridge over a stream and turn left, then right around the buildings, to cross the bridge over the River Dickler.

Alternative route:
From the bridge a bridleway to the left can be followed to Lower Swell and then by footpaths to Upper Swell. This avoids visiting Stow-on-the-Wold and three miles of lanes which follow.

From the bridge take a footpath through a gate slightly to the left. Walk up the field to a stile to the left of buildings at Netherswell Manor Farm.

Follow the track through the farm buildings and uphill through several gates. Climb steeply up a field to a coppice, where the path inclines right, leaving the coppice by a stile to a last steep field before Stow. *Most will be grateful to pause here, and to look back over route of the days walk and the extensive views. To the north is Lower Swell with Upper Swell two miles beyond. Keen eyes and a good sense of direction may identify Broadway Tower on the scarp, at least 10 miles distant.*

Turn and enter an enclosed track to the main Stow - Cirencester road. Turn left, uphill to the town, where there are shops and accommodation, including a Youth Hostel. Stow-on-the-Wold is an extremely popular tourist attraction throughout the year.

Stow-on-the-Wold – 'Where the Wind Blows Cold' - stands at 800 feet above sea level and is the highest town in Cotswold. In its heyday, 20,000 sheep were bought and sold in the market square in a single day. The church tower is prominent for many miles around.

In medieval times the Cotswolds were the centre of a great wool trade the native Cotswold sheep producing a heavy, thick fleece on land which was perfectly suited for them. Cotswold wool provided much of England's cloth, as well as a great export trade to the continent. The wool industry brought wealth to the Cotswold towns from Stroud and Cirencester to Chipping Campden, where many great manor houses and splendid churches were built out of the proceeds.

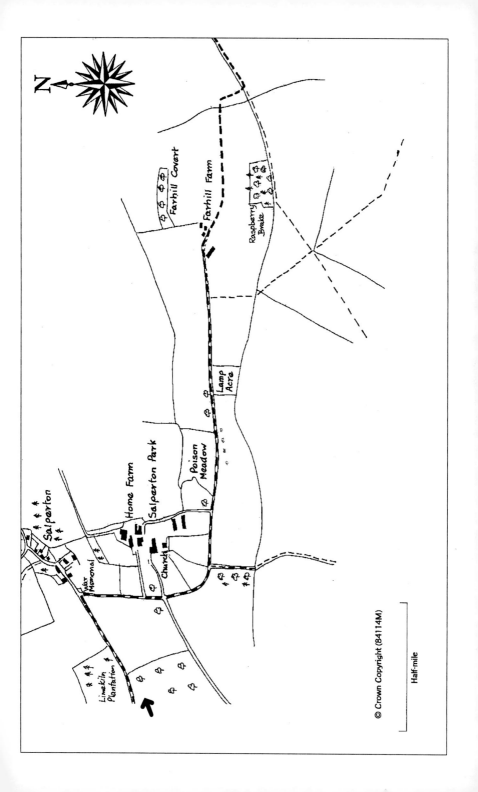

N

Salperton

Limekiln Plantation

War Memorial

Home Farm

Salperton Park

Church

Poison Meadow

Lamp Acre

Farhill Covert

Farhill Farm

Raspberry Brake

© Crown Copyright (84114M)

Half-mile

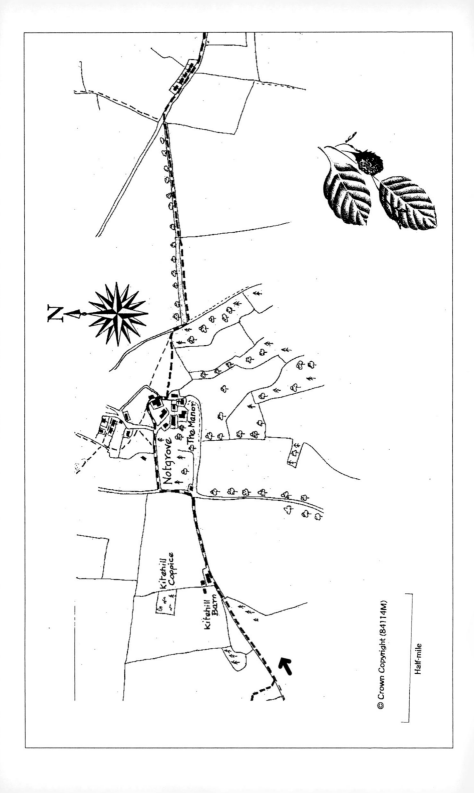

N

Notgrove

⇦The Manor

Kitehill Coppice

Kitehill Barn

© Crown Copyright (84114M)

Half-mile

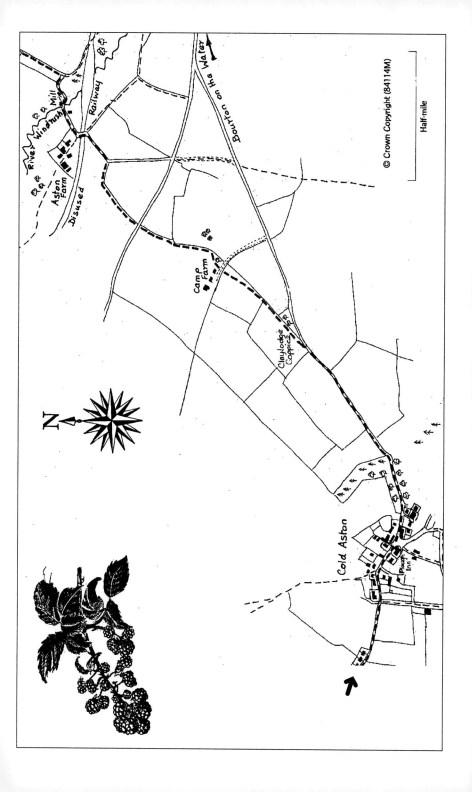

N

Half-mile

© Crown Copyright (84114M)

River Windrush

Mill

Aston Farm

Railway

Disused

Bourton on the Water

Camp Farm

Claylodge Coppice

Cold Aston

Plough Inn

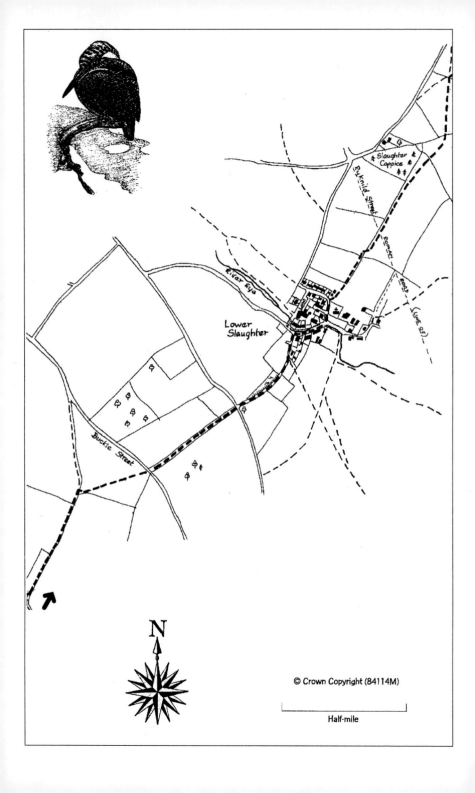

Slaughter
Coppice

Ryknild Street

Roman Road (Line of)

River Eye

Lower
Slaughter

Buckle Street

© Crown Copyright (84114M)

N

Half-mile

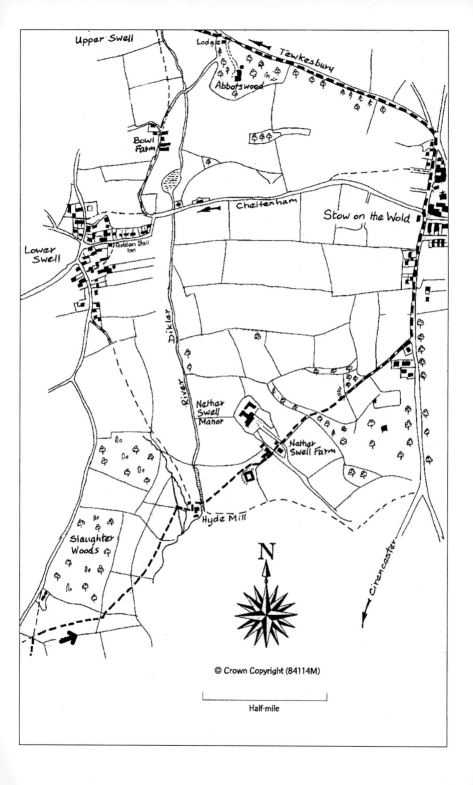

Upper Swell

Lodge

Tewkesbury

Abbotswood

Bowl Farm

Cheltenham

Stow on the Wold

Lower Swell

Golden Ball Inn

River Dikler

Nether Swell Manor

Nether Swell Farm

Hyde Mill

Slaughter Woods

Cirencester

N

© Crown Copyright (84114M)

Half-mile

Stow to Winchcombe

The next section of The Gloucestershire Way, from Stow to Winchcombe, is across splendid upland countryside. The area is extremely popular with walkers, horse riders and cyclists, and it is unfortunate that there are very few field paths to the west. Fortunately these are quiet roads with many attractions.

Leave Stow Market Square by the High Street and cross the Fosse Way at the traffic lights. Turn left on the Tewkesbury road and follow this downhill. The wide grass verge is usually well mown and preferable to walking on the road. Turn left onto a footpath near the entrance to Abbotswood House. Follow the fence line down to cross the River Dickler by a stone bridge. Walk up the enclosed field edge beyond and, ignoring the path to the left, turn right through a gate to cross the paddocks to the road. Turn left uphill into the hamlet of Upper Swell, being careful of the traffic approaching around the sharp bends.

The area between Stow and Upper Swell was once tree-covered, and it was said that 'a squirrel could hop from Stow to Swell without resting his foot or wetting his toe.

Leaving Upper Swell, turn right on the lane to Donnington. Drop down to cross the Dickler again and then climb past the entrance to Donnington brewery.

Originally a corn mill, the brewery has been worked continuously by the Arkle family since 1865. The Dickler rises on the estate and drove the water wheels for the brewery's power up to 1959.

At the T-junction turn left towards Condicote. After a mile or so along this high upland road, turn right and shortly enter the village.

It is worth walking around the ancient village green to view the wayside cross. This is set alongside a spring which sustained the inhabitants, and many weary travellers at this important junction of ancient ways, over the centuries.

Condicote is a bleak spot in winter and usually breezy in mid-summer, one wonders how it came to attract the first settlers. But in the right mood or weather the atmosphere of antiquity is tangible. With its 600 year old wayside cross, prehistoric henges and ancient trackways, Condicote is both Cotswold and Gloucestershire history.

Follow the lane northwest out of Condicote, crossing the line of our old friend Ryknild Street. Continue along this ancient track for a mile to a T-junction.

Alternative route:
Cross straight over the T-junction into woodland. On reaching the open field follow the wood edge to the left and then cross fields to pass between the farm buildings. The footpath turns right beyond the barns and continues uphill to converge with a track alongside a boundary wall. After about 100 yards the path passes through a gap in the wall, and then crosses the next field diagonally, passing immediately left of a circular clump of trees. Pass through a gap in a wall and follow parallel to the woodland on the left, until an obvious track descends the short slope through woodland and past a lake at the bottom. Follow the valley up to Trafalgar Farm. From the house the footpath crosses a small

paddock to the farm buildings, but walkers are encouraged to use the farm drive to the farm buildings and continue past these to reach the road. Turn left over Trafalgar Crossroads. After just over half a mile turn right onto a bridleway and follow this ancient track down into Temple Guiting, where there is a post office and village shop. Turn left on the village street and follow this down to the River Windrush. (The alternative route from the Plough Inn at Ford joins by a track on the right just before reaching the river.)

Walk up to a T-junction and turn right to a footpath on the left after about 200 yards. Follow this headland path uphill before descending at the edge of woodland to Pinnock Farm, a medieval village site. Cross a stream and walk up the track, past the farm entrance and follow an enclosed path up to the road, to join the main route of The Gloucestershire Way.

Turn right, and after 160 yards, left on a bridleway track into woodland. Emerging into open fields a footpath keeps straight ahead, but The Gloucestershire Way turns left following the bridleway to the right of the hedge. Nearing the next boundary, the bridleway angles to the right across the corner of the field to a gateway then continues across the next field to the remains of Botany Barn.

The bridleway continues on the same line through young woodland, but The Gloucestershire Way forks left at this point onto a track beside a wall. *This open ridge-top provides a great sense of kinship with the early people who once traversed these tracks. The spreading prospect of Cotswold to the north, particularly during the winter months, reveals many ancient farmsteads close to the line of Ryknild Street.* Follow this open ridge-top for about a mile to Ford Hill Farm, and continue up to Buckle Street, last crossed at Lower Slaughter.

Cross the road into a racehorse training establishment at Jackdaws Castle.

STOW TO WINCHCOMBE

Follow the main track, but where the public path has recently been diverted, take particular note of the warning signs displayed where the footpath crosses the gallops. Follow the track downhill to the road at Ford and welcome refreshment at the Plough Inn.

Alternative route:
From the Plough Inn an attractive diversion may be made through Temple Guiting and the site of a medieval village at Pinnock. Turn left along the road to Stow, using the grass verge for safety, to a footpath on the right after about a quarter of a mile. Follow this into Temple Guiting, where the alternative path from Condicote is joined.

From the Plough Inn turn right (left if you are emerging from the pub) and walk downhill to cross the infant River Windrush, which rises a short distance to the north at Taddington Barn. This narrow section of road needs special care because of the danger from fast moving traffic. Continue up to a junction and turn left towards Temple Guiting. Within a few paces turn right and follow a footpath uphill, keeping the hedgerow on the left. Just over the hill crest reach a cross boundary along the top of quarry workings and turn left. Walk down an attractive hollow path under trees, and then open fields, to the farm buildings at Slade Barn.

Turn left onto the narrow upland road and follow this winding uphill. After quarter of a mile pass the entrance to a path on the left which is the alternative route from Condicote and Temple Guiting. Over the top of the hill is a junction with a narrow lane to Farmcote, an ancient community. *Less obvious is Campden Lane descending from the high ground between thick hedges. This is part of the old Cotswold Ridgeway, the ancient Jurassic Way running from Yorkshire down to the ancient monuments of Wiltshire and beyond.*

THE GLOUCESTERSHIRE WAY

Roel Gate

I love to walk the secret ways of prehistoric man,
Where scratched across the Cotswold Hills the ancient trackways ran.
The cattle ways, the salt ways, the lonely pilgrims ride
To the hinterland of England from silver Severnside.

I wonder if these ancient folk had time to stand and stare,
Saw beauty in the rolling hills and loved the upland air;
Gazed eastward over English plains to watch the morning rise,
Or lingered long on Birdlip Hill to gaze at sunset skies.

Perhaps they made these upland ways with nothing more in mind
Than to escape the hazards of the plains they left behind.
But glad I am they ran them on skylines lifted high
Where we may walk on quiet hills beneath a Cotswold sky.

And best of all, the ancient way that climbs by Salter's Hill
To ride a world of sky and wind where time is standing still.
Here by the lonely Roel Gate where fields fade into sky,
Here on the roof of Cotswold I touch eternity.

Arthur Dalby

Turn left and follow this ancient way to the junction at Lynes Barn
Farm and shortly afterwards leave the road at the second of two footpaths
on the right. Walk down to a barn and 150 yards after a gate fork left off
the track into woodland. Emerge from the woodland and walk on the
level along a fine sweeping belvedere towards Little Farmcote. *The ever-
widening view of the Cotswold edge includes Farmcote on the opposite
ridge with Beckbury hillfort high above the hamlet.* From Little Farmcote
follow the left fork in the farm road to cross the old saltway, which
climbs up from the vale before crossing Cotswold to the River Thames.

This is not the original saltway. Winchcombe Abbey owned salt rights

92

at Droitwich several centuries before Hailes Abbey was built in the 12th Century. The old British saltway would have gone directly to Winchcombe via Toddington, where the old route was changed with the realignment of roads in the 18th Century.

Mediaeval salt carriers were not the pioneers of these saltways. Facing long journeys through wet and wooded country, with heavily laden animals, they would have used the most direct of the network of tracks spreading over Cotswold, first trodden out by prehistoric people. Deviations from these tracks connected many of the manors owning salt rights at Droitwich.

Cross the lane and walk up two fields to a gate on the skyline. Turn left and cross a stile into a small coppice. *The climb over the stile and the steep contour provide a good excuse to stop and catch your breath. Looking out over the vale, Hailes, with its 12th century church and ruined abbey, is tucked into a fold in the foreground. This spot is shown on the old maps as Monk's Hole. Not knowing the reason for this it might be surmised that medieval peasantry looking down at the Abbey may have muttered 'B***** monks in their hole'! A more mundane explanation may be that a penitent monk established a hermit's cell hereabouts.*

Beyond the coppice is an area of scrub often overgrown with blackthorn and bramble, but usually with a path winding through. Find a way from the stile for about 50 yards before turning right to descend the steep slope, through more hawthorn and brambles. At the foot of the slope cross a boundary fence and continue downhill over open grassland, with a wall to the right, shown as Fluke's Hill on the map. After about 300 yards go through a bridle gate in the wall.

Beyond, incline slightly left and descend steeply, sometimes very muddy and slippery, through hawthorn and blackthorn. As the slope lessens walk down through fields to reach Stancombe Lane. Cross this and walk down to a gate to the right of the farm house. Cross the farm drive to a further gate and pass to the right of a barn. Walk down a further field to a lane on the outskirts of Winchcombe. Turn left and immediately right through a kissing gate and cross the meadow to an enclosed path between cottages. Emerge into Castle Street and turn right over the River Isbourne and then walk up into the town.

Of the Cotswold streams, the Isbourne is the odd one out, in flowing north to the Avon and the Severn valley, whereas the others all flow east as tributaries to the Thames.

Winchcombe, as befits the ancient capital of Mercia, has an atmosphere of antiquity more so than any other Cotswold town. King Offa, responsible for the National Monument along the Welsh Border, was King of Mercia in AD 794. His son, Kenulf, commenced the building of the Abbey which was dedicated by Wulfred, Archbishop of Canterbury, assisted by 12 other bishops in AD 811. There are no visible remains of the Abbey today and the site is hidden from view behind the high wall and Holm oaks along Abbey Terrace.

In 1485 the Abbot commenced the restoration of the ruinous Parish church in order to discourage the populace from worshipping in his Abbey. The townspeople were unable to raise sufficient funds to continue the project which was completed at the expense of Lord Sudeley. At the Dissolution a few years later, the townspeople preferred to raise the money to purchase their Parish Church of St. Peter: rather than the Abbey. Unlike the inhabitants of Tewkesbury and Pershore who saved their abbeys from destruction.

Winchcombe attracts walkers from far and wide and is probably as popular as any other centre in the Cotswolds. As a result there is plenty of accommodation, cafés and pubs and good car parking. The reason for this popularity is not hard to find. The proximity of Cotswold, with numerous pretty villages along the edge, and Cleeve Hill, highest point in the county rising nearby, provide splendid walking country radiating out from the town. Various guidebooks are available which do justice to the walking in the Winchcombe vicinity.

The Cotswold Way, proposed National Trail, passes through the town where walkers can take a break on their journey between Chipping Campden and Bath.

The Wychavon Way, runs for 40 miles north from Winchcombe, over Bredon Hill and into the Worcestershire countryside to Droitwich.

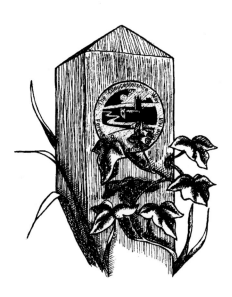

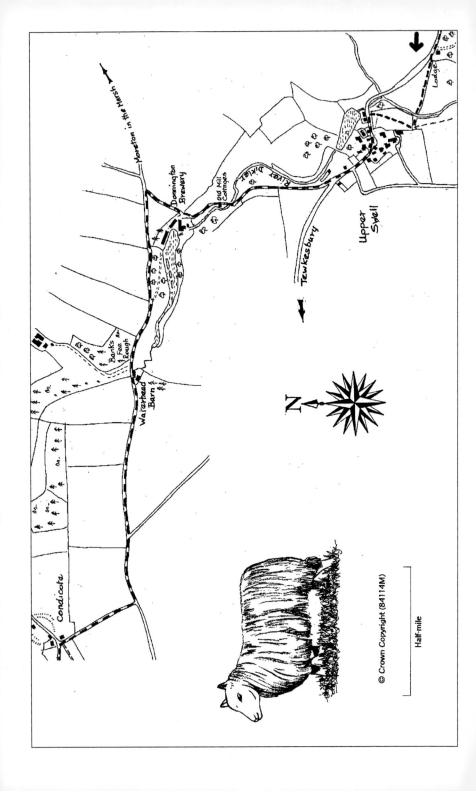

Moreton in the Marsh

Donnington Brewery

Old Mill Cottages

River Dikler

Tewkesbury

Upper Swell

Lodge

Banks or Foa Rough

Warcarhead Barn

Condicote

N

© Crown Copyright (84114M)

Half-mile

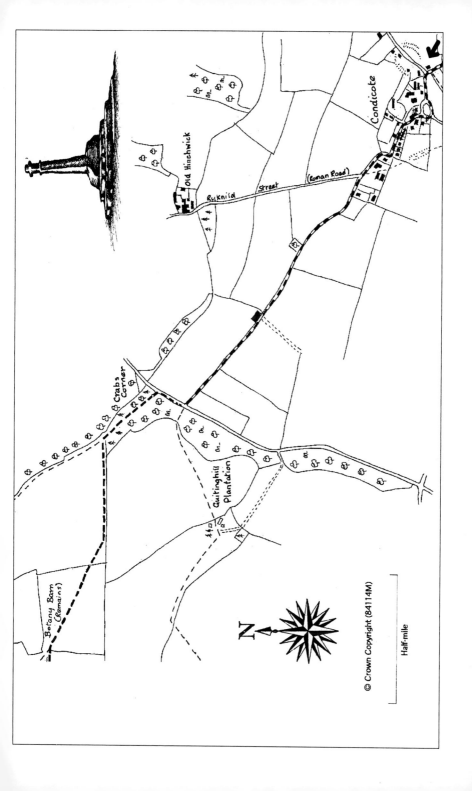

Condicote

Old Hinchwick

Ruknild Street (Conan Road)

Crabs Corner

Guitinghill Plantation

Botany Barn (Remains)

N

© Crown Copyright (84114M)

Half-mile

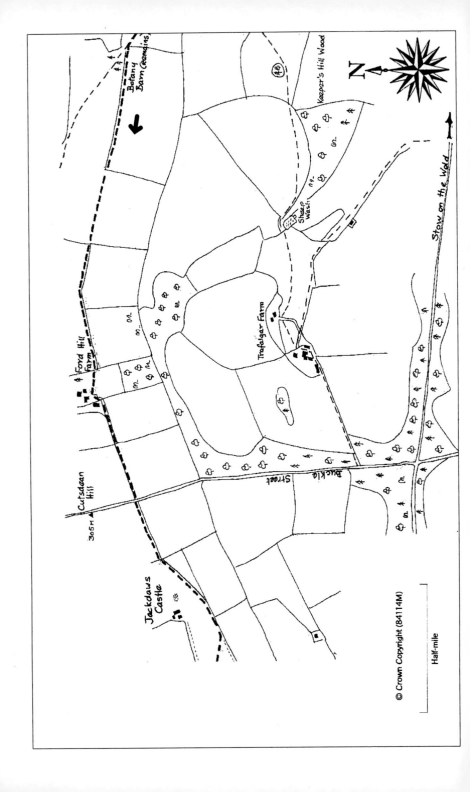

N

Stow on the Wold

Keeper's Hill Wood

Botany Barn (Remains)

Sheep Wash

Ford Hill Farm

Trafalgar Farm

Cutsdean Hill

305m

Buckle Street

Jackdaws Castle

© Crown Copyright (84114M)

Half-mile

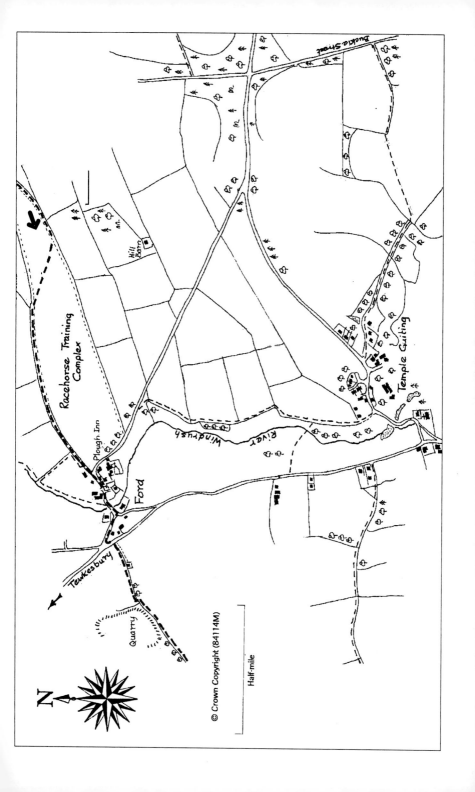

N

Buckle Street

Temple Guiting

Racehorse Training Complex

Hill Barn

Plough Inn

Ford

Windrush River

Tewkesbury

Quarry

© Crown Copyright (84114M)

Half-mile

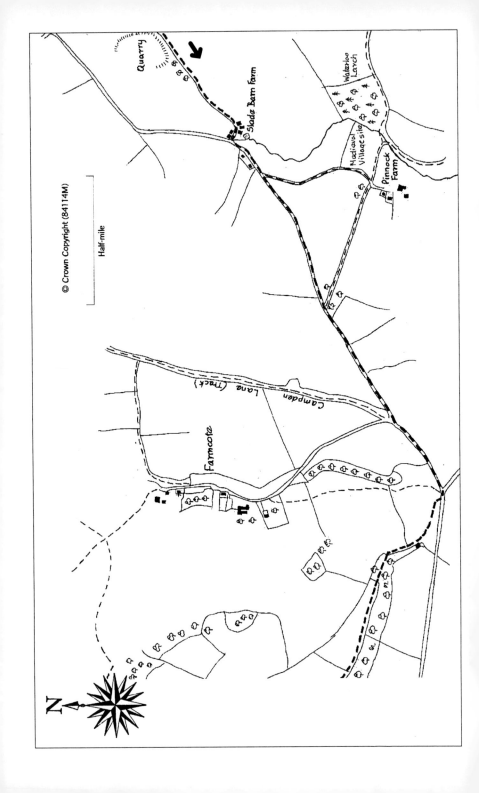

© Crown Copyright (84114M)

Half-mile

Quarry

Slade Barn Farm

Waterloo Larch

Medieval Village site

Pinnock Farm

Campden Lane (Track)

Farmcote

N

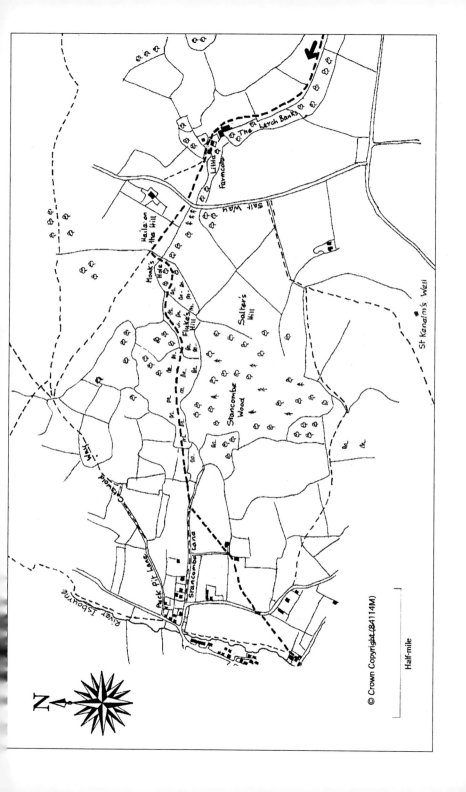

The Larch Banks

Linha
Farmcote

Salt Way

Hailes on the Hill

Monk's
Hale

St Kanaim's Well

Fluke's Hill

Salter's Hill

Stancombe Wood

Halel

Pack Pit Lane

Stancombe Lane

River Isbourne

© Crown Copyright (84114M)

Half-mile

N

Winchcombe to Tewkesbury

From Winchcombe The Gloucestershire Way coincides with the Wychavon Way for a short distance over Langley Hill. Leave the town via Gloucester Street, passing the massive Norman church of St. Peter's, and at the ancient Corner Cupboard Inn, once a farmhouse, turn right. At a junction turn left and fork right into Harvey's Lane. Walk up, ever steepening, for about a quarter of a mile, passing the entrance to Enfield Farm, a cottage and a cattle grid and then turn right over a stile.

The path climbs steeply up the slopes of Langley Hill to a corner with a stone slab stile. Continue uphill over short, springy turf to a track alongside a wall. This is shortly joined by a further track from the left. After 50 yards this track turns sharply down to the right while The Gloucestershire Way continues on a level track which soon descends slightly. *The changing view includes Alderton and Dumbleton Hills, which form an attractive group with a fine backdrop provided by Bredon Hill, over the Worcestershire border.*

Near the ruins of old farm buildings the waymark posts indicate the Wychavon Way continuing to the right down to Gretton. The Gloucestershire Way keeps well to the left through a field gate. Ignore a footpath to the left and continue, with the steep slope to the left, up to a small gate in a wall. The path levels and the views extend over the Severn Vale to the Malvern Hills.

I'm homesick for my hills again
My hills again!
To see above the Severn plain
Unscabbarded against the sky
The blue high blade of Cotswold lie;
The giant clouds go royally
By jagged Malvern with a train
Of shadows. Where the land is low
Like a huge imprisoning O
I hear a heart that's sound and high,
I hear the heart within me Cry:
'I'm homesick for my hills again
My hills again!
Cotswold or Malvern, sun or rain
My hills again!'

F W Harvey

The path joins a bridleway and turns right descending steeply to a small plateau and a crosstrack. Continue straight over, using a gate on the left, and cross the plateau to the right of a barn. The bridleway follows a sunken track down to the hamlet of Far Stanley. The last section can be wet and boggy in winter, and it may be better to climb out of the track and walk down the field to the bridlegate at the bottom. After a second bridlegate turn right through the stableyard and then follow the road down, under the railway, to a junction. Turn left down to a sharp bend and leave the road through a bridlegate straight ahead.

This large field, although disfigured by electricity pylons, is worthy of note, being recorded in an historical painting as Alderton Parish Hay Meadow. It is well worth viewing the field from the slopes of Dixton Hill and then, if you are able, visit Cheltenham Art Gallery to compare the scene with the painting. Every hedgerow and topographical feature exist as depicted 250 years ago (see Appendix 3).

The bridleway winds up and around the shoulder of Dixton Hill past the manor, and down to the road. At the junction turn left and take the bridleway on the right after a few yards. Walk down to a gateway and continue across a wide field, crossing a rivulet from a spring, to a hedgerow and larger stream. Walkers can avoid the bridlegate and muddy ford by a stile and footbridge on the left. From here either the footpath or bridleway can be followed. The bridleway being more direct to Woolstone Farm, but is sometimes wet and heavy going. The footpath contours to the left further down the hillside, across three fields. Descend a fourth field to join another bridleway and turn right to Woolstone Farm.

Walk up the road for about 200 yards and immediately after Crane Hill Farm take a footpath on the right, climbing steeply uphill. Towards the top, the path keeps to the left following the hedge and then circles behind the hill to a stile. *The views from Crane Hill are extensive. To the south, Gloucester and the cathedral can be seen over the village of Gotherington. West, over Oxenton village, Tewkesbury lies in the Severn Vale where, in good light, the Abbey is prominent. The Malvern Hills may beckon the more ambitious walker and a link, to The Worcestershire Way, is described in the next chapter.*

Continue uphill to a stile under a large ash tree in the corner. From the stile the public path through Picklechurch Brake is obstructed by barbed wire fences, and the landowner has created a path along the left hand boundary at the edge of a coppice. Leave the coppice through a gate and turn left on a farm track which curves downhill to the left and then right. The footpath cuts across the bend to a gateway in the lower boundary fence, and joins a farm track down to Oxenton.

Walking down the village street past the church and attractive gardens, there is an awareness of leaving the high blue hills and beginning the final stage of The Gloucestershire Way.

Leaving Oxenton, cross the Cheltenham - Evesham road through a gate and follow the headland path alongside spacious fields. *Behind, Crane Hill and Woolstone Hill still loom closely, and the great whaleback of Bredon Hill fills the northern horizon. Across the fields in front the tower of Tewkesbury Abbey stands out against the backdrop of the Malvern Hills.*

After a gate the hedge on the right ends abruptly. Cross the field to a stile in the hedge and then cross a smaller field to a stile to the right of a gate leading onto a green lane.

Starveall Lane, a name indicative perhaps of unproductive land, is wide, hedged and straight, ends abruptly in a nearby field. This may be explained by the large area of woodland revealed on old maps at that point.

Cross Starveall Lane slightly left through a gate and follow the hedge on the left, through two gates to Claydon Farm. A short length of enclosed track leads to a lane which is followed for 100 yards to a stile on the right.

Alternative route
To avoid crossing the railway, walk down the lane and over the bridge. At a crossroad continue straight on down a wide grass bridleway. All too soon this pleasant bridleway joins a road which is then followed over the motorway. After 300 yards turn left onto another old track past Chapel Farm. At the next junction rejoin the road and at a sharp bend turn left through a gate.

Follow the hedge for a short distance through a gate into an old perry orchard. Immediately before the next gate from the orchard, turn left over a stile. At the hedge corner, within a few paces, walk diagonally right across the field to a stile and footbridge over the Tirle Brook.

From the bridge turn right alongside the hedge and at the corner continue across the wide field, on the same line, to a further stile. *This slightly elevated position gives fine views back to Cotswold with the high point of Cleeve Hill prominent. Much of the blue Cotswold edge is hidden behind the outlying hills, including wooded Langley Hill and bare Crane Hill, recently crossed.*

After the stile the footpath gradually converges with a hedge on the left to join a track from a house. Follow this down to the T-junction. Turn left and cross the railway with extreme care. Walk down to a road junction and straight on for a few yards. Where the road bends left continue straight over passing a post box and a cottage, into an attractive green bridleway.

This ends all too soon and civilisation looms in the form of the noisy M5 motorway with, a little incongruously, the ancient tower of Tewkesbury Abbey beyond. Over the motorway, turn right after the second gate. Follow the headland to a pond, then left along the headland track to a gate onto an enclosed track which leads into the village of Walton Cardiff. At the road turn right and follow a sharp bend past the manor house to a junction. Continue left past a pond and at the apex of the bend cross over to a gate on the right where the alternative route from Claydon Farm rejoins. *This was the site of an old chapel giving its name to several features in the area, including Chapel Farm.*

Follow the hedge and stream for about 50 yards and cross the field diagonally to a footbridge. Two surviving willow trees indicate the water course which the footpath once followed. From the bridge follow the hedgerow for a short distance to a stile, and cross the next meadow diagonally left on a line to the right of the Abbey tower. Reaching the far hedge walk left round a corner to a stile hidden from view. Cross and turn left to a further stile into a driveway, follow this for a short distance and cross Tirle Brook again. Turn left and follow the brook alongside houses. Passing the confluence with Swilgate Brook. At the road cross over through a childrens' play area to Swilgate Road and follow this to Tewkesbury Abbey and the Town Centre.

The massive tower of Tewkesbury Abbey rises prominently out of the floodplain and dominates the approach to the town from all directions. In good light the tower is visible for many miles from The Gloucestershire Way.

Tewkesbury's position, at the confluence of the Avon and Severn, means that the floodplain still fills regularly during the winter months. The final stages of our walk crosses the willow-lined tributaries of Tirle Brook and Swilgate, two of a maze of waterways around the town.

Robert Fitzhamon raised the present Abbey in about 1200, bringing some of the stone from his native Caen in Normandy, that being easier to transport by water than the local stone was by the roads. Three hundred years later the townspeople saved their Abbey from destruction by paying the sum of £453 to Henry VIII at the Dissolution.

Tewkesbury is an attractive town where tourism is increasing rapidly. The Abbey has many visitors throughout the year but the town is also well endowed with many medieval buildings threaded by a number of alleyways worth exploring. The Battle of Tewkesbury was the culmination of the Wars of the Roses, when the Lancastrians, led by Queen Margaret and the young Prince of Wales, were routed by Yorkist forces. Bloody Meadow can be visited on the town's 'Battle Trail'. Additionally, there are several hotels with historic connections. The Abbey Mill and Bell Hotel appear in Mrs. Craig's 'John Halifax Gentleman', Dickens had Mr. Pickwick visit the Hop Pole Hotel, whilst Shakespeare's Falstaff thought highly of Tewkesbury mustard.

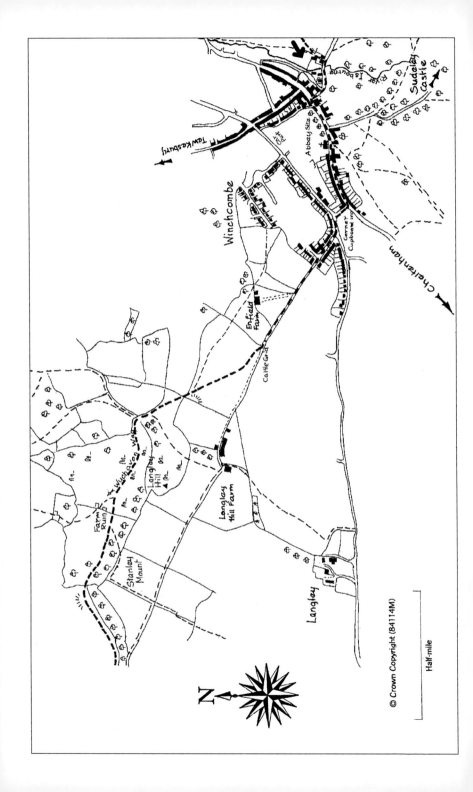

Sudeley Castle

River Isbourne

Tewkesbury

Abbey Site

Winchombe

Corner Cupboard Inn

Cheltenham

Enfield Farm

Cattle Grid

Wichavon Way

Langley Hill

Stanley Mount

Farm Ruin

Langley Hill Farm

Langley

© Crown Copyright (B4114M)

Half-mile

N

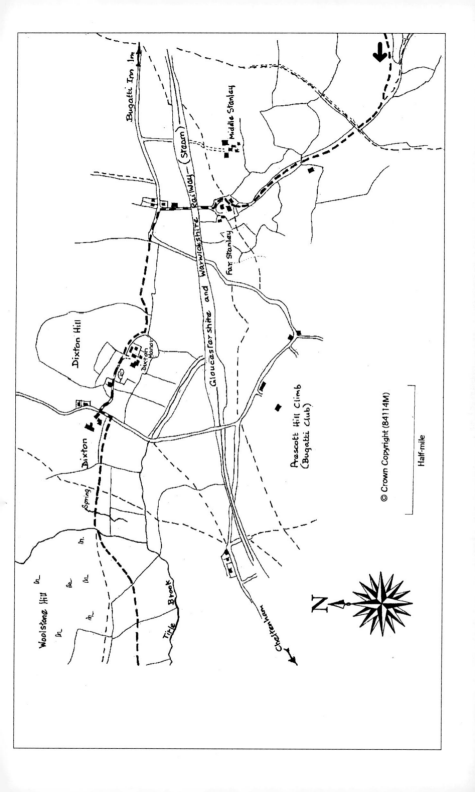

Woolstone Hill

Dixton Hill

Bugatti Inn Inn

Middle Stanley

Dixton

Dixton Manor

Spring

Gloucestershire and Warwickshire Railway (Steam)

Far Stanley

Tirle Brook

Cheltenham

Prescott Hill Climb
(Bugatti Club)

N

© Crown Copyright (84114M)

Half-mile

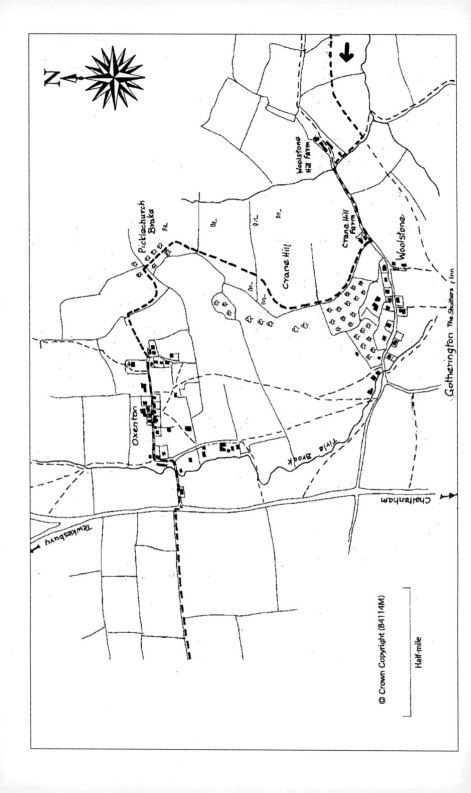

N

Woolstone Hill Farm

Picklechurch Brake

Crane Hill

Crane Hill Farm

Woolstone

Oxenton

Gotherington The Shutters / Inn

Tirle Brook

Cheltenham

Tewkesbury

© Crown Copyright (84114M)

Half-mile

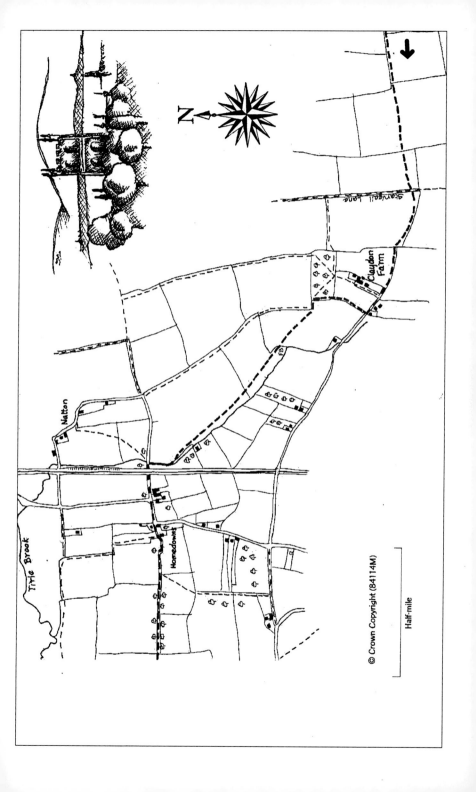

Tytle Brook

Natton

Homedowns

Granval Lane

Claydon Farm

N

© Crown Copyright (84114M)

Half-mile

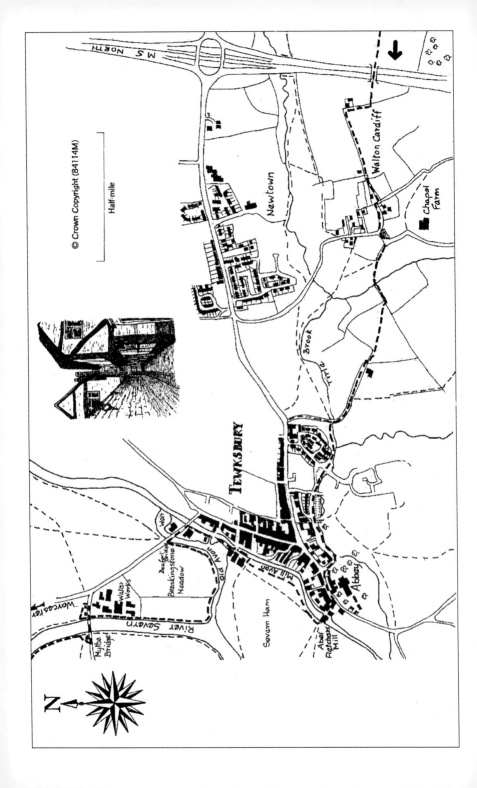

© Crown Copyright (84114M)

Half-mile

N

M5 NORTH

Walton Cardiff

Chapel Farm

Newtown

Little Brook

TEWKSBURY

Worcester

Mythe Bridge

Water Works

Bridge Brockingstone Meadow

Old Avon

River Severn

Severn Ham

Mill Avon

Weir

Abel Fletchers Mill

Abbey

The Worcestershire Way Link

This is a pleasant walk linking The Gloucestershire Way to The Worcestershire Way on the Malvern Hills. Northwards The Worcestershire Way links with The Staffordshire Way and several other long paths into the Midlands and Wales.

<u>Alternative route</u>:
Walk through the Abbey grounds and some of the medieval alleyways to reach St John's Bridge over the River Avon.

From the Abbey, cross the road and walk down the narrow street alongside the Old Bell Hotel. Cross the Avon by a footway at the Abbey Mill shared with the Severn Way, now extended to link with the Worcestershire section on the west bank of the Severn. Turn right on the floodbank until obliged to re-cross the Avon by a modern bridge. Turn left and within a few yards cross again, this time by the Mill Bridge, and follow the riverside path over the lock gate to reach the road at St John's Bridge.

There are two bridges, King John's Bridge over the Mill Avon, was according to legend, built on King John's orders. A bridge is known to have existed here in 1205 and parts of ribbed arches still remain. Beaufort Bridge over the old Avon, was rebuilt in 1962 with a single arch. King John's was widened at that time with new stone work on the south side whilst the north side remains unaltered.

113

Turn left over Beaufort Bridge and take the footpath immediately on the left. This circuitous route around Breakingstone Meadow is preferable to walking alongside the busy road, although this will sometimes be necessary when the meadow is under water during the winter months. The path follows the old Avon to the junction with the Severn, and within sight of our starting point at the Abbey Mill. Alongside the Severn the footpath enters Mythe waterworks and is carried over the intake by an expensive stainless steel walkway to exit under the arches of Mythe Bridge. Continue across a lawn and at the path junction beyond turn right and, after a few yards, right again up steps to the road.

Mythe Bridge was also built by Thomas Telford and completed in 1827.

Cross Mythe Bridge to the tollhouse on the Worcestershire side of the Severn. Take the footpath on the right and follow the riverbank for a mile and a quarter. Where electricity pylons converge with the river, turn left onto a farm track which turns back to a junction with a lane. Turn sharp right uphill to Moss Green Kennels. Follow the track to the left, passing cottages and continue on the headland path. At the first hedge boundary deviate half left, away from the headland, to a stile. Continue across the next field and rejoin the headland at the corner of the woodland on the right. Follow the edge of the wood through a second hedge boundary. A few yards beyond, the woodland bends away to the right, continue over the field to a gate onto a lane at Bushley Green.

Follow the lane for a few yards and where this bends left, continue across the grass at the edge of the woodland, then through scattered trees, to a road junction. Cross to a bridleway track which soon turns right and is enclosed between hedges. After passing under an arch emerge into open fields. Walk down on the same line to a gate and then along a headland track to join a lane at Guller's End. Pass a redbrick farmhouse and follow the road around to the left. At the sharp left bend take the track down to the right and under the M50 motorway.

Turn left and follow the track as it curves to the right through a gate. At the next gate continue straight on along the headland, ignoring a footpath on the left to Chambers Court. After the next stile, pass to the left of a dew pond immediately in front and descend to a footbridge over a stream. *There are extensive views from the dew pond to the Malvern Hills and the Severn plain to the north. The spire of Longdon church is prominent in the foreground.* From the bridge walk up to a stile and keep left of the hedge in front. The path changes to the opposite side of the hedge after 150 yards. Follow the headland into Longdon, where the churchyard is a pleasant place to pause for a few minutes with the Plough Inn nearby for refreshments.

Leaving the village past the pub, ignore a road to the left. Walk down to a sharp right bend and turn left into an enclosed bridleway track. This curves to the right along the contour, giving a wide view over Longdon Marsh to the Malvern ridge. The track drops down left, and at the bottom of the slope, turn right for a short distance before crossing Bushley Brook by a farm bridge. Follow the headland track with the hedge on your left along the foot of Coney Burrow Hill.

After a gate continue along the headland, this time with the hedge on the right, and pass through another gate in an angle of the same hedge. *A footpath off to the right leads up to Eastington Hall, an Elizabethan manor house. On the nearer hill is an attractive brick and timber field barn.* Continue along the hedge until it turns off to the left. Walk across the field on the same line to a gate, and continue past a cattle trough to a footbridge alongside a willow tree. Climb the slope in front towards the buildings of Orchard Farm. *There are excellent views back to Longdon church and, in the gap to the left of Coney Burrow Hill, the blue outline of Oxenton and Langley Hills traversed by The Gloucestershire Way.*

Climb an awkward stile and cross to the farmyard. Pass through the gates and farm buildings and then past houses to reach a road. Cross directly to a gate, and walk down the slope of the long field to a bridle gate. Walk over the next field to the right of a white cottage and cross a lane through two gates. Walk up a headland with the hedge on the right, over a stile, erected alongside the old pedestrian gate, and down to a bridge and lake at Mill Brook. Follow the track uphill to join a road.

Passing Welland Court continue on the road for a short distance to a junction. Bear left, crossing the grass triangle and follow the lane to the left. Past farm buildings the lane becomes a track. Where this bends to the left, just before the entrance to a waterworks, turn through a gate on the right and cross the field to a footbridge. Continue over the next field to a stile and gate and cross a track to a further gate. Follow the hedge on the right uphill to reach a gate out of sight until the last moment. Do not pass through this but turn left along the hedge to a gate and continue to a further gate and a stile in the corner. Pass through and turn right through a small paddock to a high stile into an orchard. Follow the ditch on the right and join a track from a cottage. Pass through a gate and continue on the track. After crossing a road follow a footpath over Castlemorton Common.

Cross a further road and continue on the same line to join a lane at a bridge. Cross the bridge, either turn left and walk up the Common, or follow the lane as it bends sharply left, to reach a second bridge over this and continue, passing cottages and bungalows on the right. About 300 yards from the bridge reach a gate, usually closed, across the road. Turn left before the gate, over a small footbridge, and follow a track alongside the hedge towards the ridge of the Malvern Hills. The track passes through a narrow enclosed area for about 100 yards, but after a gate, follow a boundary fence on the left, uphill.

At a corner cross a stile and turn right up the steep open hillside to a level area and a cross track. Over this, inclining slightly left under power cables, cross a green track. Continue up a narrow path to the left above the power lines. This path steepens considerably for a time before levelling and dropping down to a white cottage in a hollow. Turn right, uphill, for 100 yards to join the Malvern ridge.

The walker with time to spare may wish to turn right and continue northwards to complete The Worcestershire Way before joining The Staffordshire Way and Cheshire Gritstone Trail.

To avoid backtracking at the end of this link The Gloucestershire Way walkers may arrange transport from the car park at Hollybush. Continuing the link for the two miles, southwards, to Hollybush is strongly recommended.

Turn left and climb the ridge for no more than 150 yards. With the ridge still climbing ahead, ensure that you turn right down a narrow green path through the gorse. This descends under trees to join a track. After about a mile cross a major track, the right hand branch climbing to the Obelisk on Midsummer Hill.

Our path continues climbing uphill and during the next half mile gives splendid views to the south and west, with the Obelisk prominent and Eastnor Castle visible down in the trees to the left. May Hill, traversed in the early part of The Gloucestershire Way, is on the horizon to the south and in between, with good visibility, the hills and woods of south Herefordshire with a backdrop of the Sugar Loaf, Skirrid and the long ridge of the Black Mountains.

Continue down the track which becomes a surfaced lane to the car park at Hollybush and the termination of the Worcestershire Way.

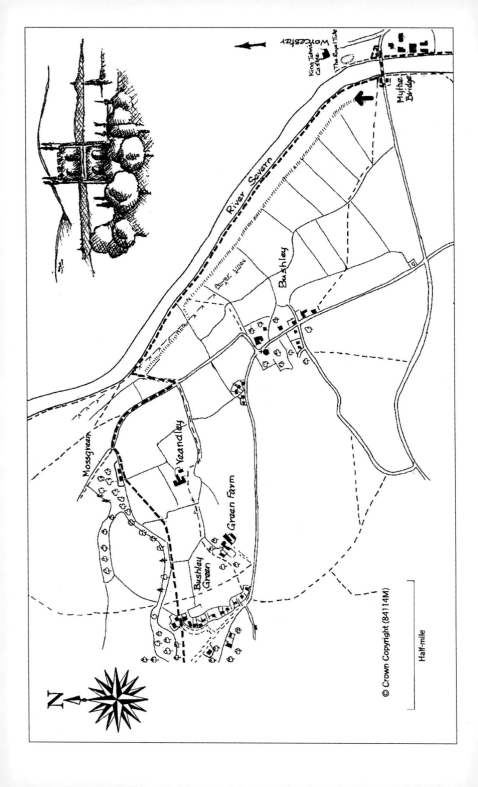

River Severn

Worcester

King John's Castle

The Bunch of Tute

Mythe Bridge

Power Lines

Bushley

Mossqveen

Yeandley

Green Farm

Bushley Green

© Crown Copyright (84114M)

Half-mile

N

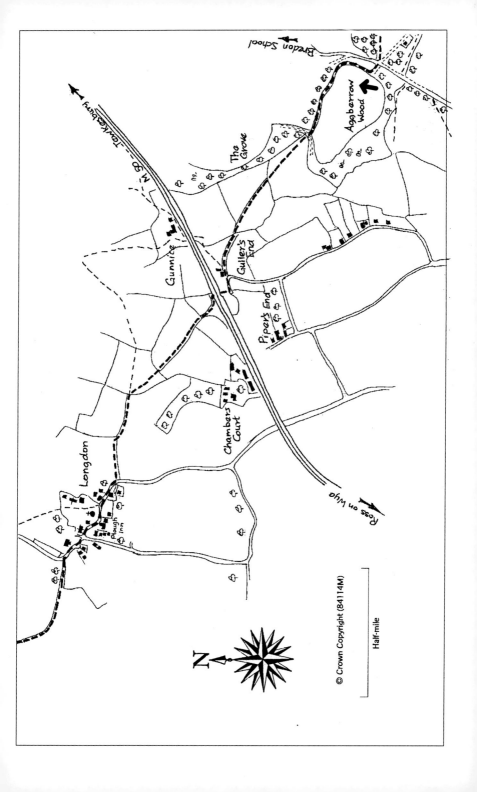

© Crown Copyright (84114M)

Half-mile

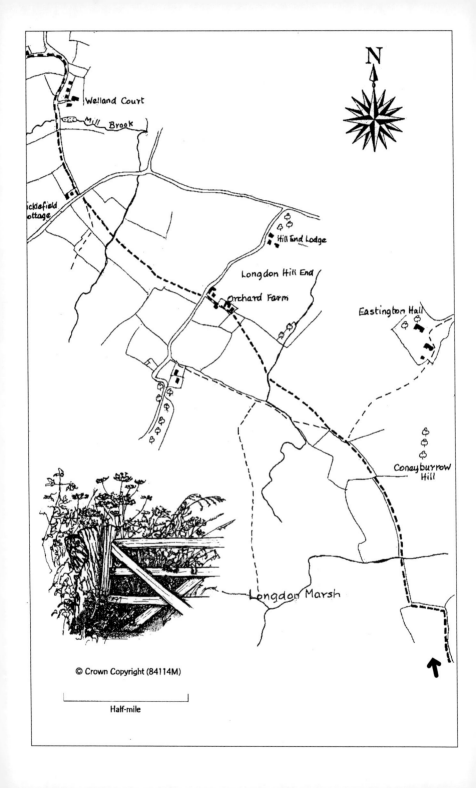

N

Welland Court

Mill Brook

icklefield
ottage

Hill End Lodge

Longdon Hill End

Orchard Farm

Eastington Hall

Conayburrow
Hill

Longdon Marsh

© Crown Copyright (84114M)

Half-mile

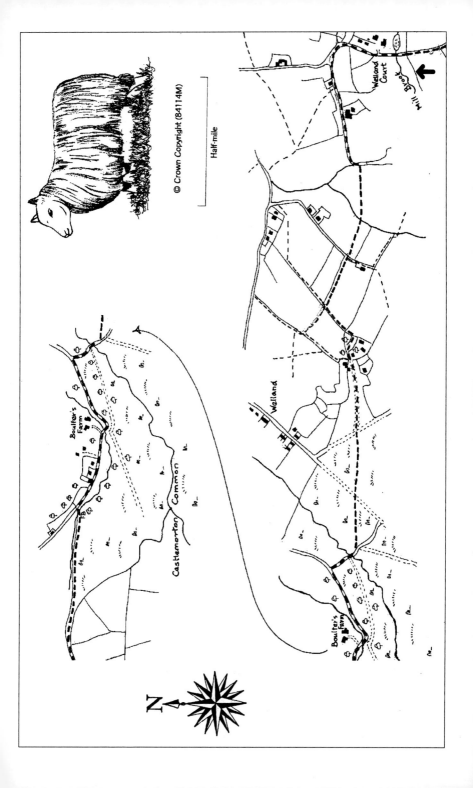

© Crown Copyright (84114M)

Half-mile

Welland Court

Mill Brook

Boulter's Farm

Castlemorton Common

N

Welland

Boulter's Farm

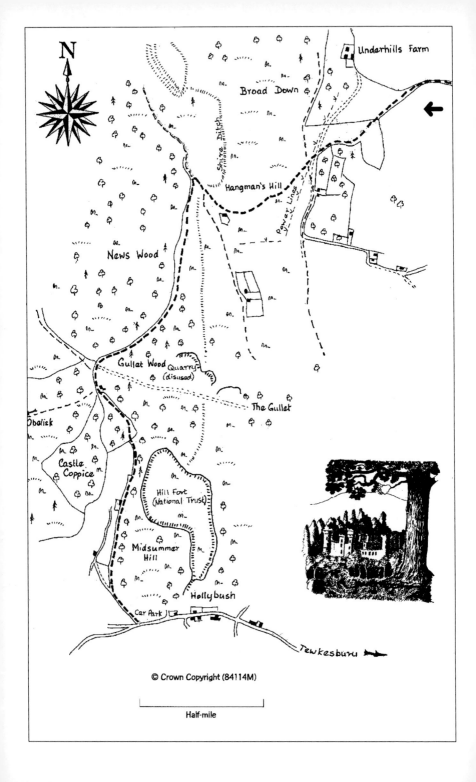

N

Underhills Farm

Broad Down

Shire Ditch

Hangman's Hill

Power Lines

News Wood

Gullat Wood Quarry
(disused)

The Gullat

Obelisk

Castle
Coppice

Hill Fort
(National Trust)

Midsummer
Hill

Hollybush

Car Park

Tewkesbury

© Crown Copyright (84114M)

Half-mile

Appendix 1

About a quarter of The Gloucestershire Way passes through the geographical area administered by Forest of Dean District Council. A large proportion of the area is heavily wooded, based on the Old Statutory Forest, but with added woodland on the periphery. Owned by the Forestry Commission and currently administered by Forest Enterprise, much of the peripheral woodland is accessible by public rights of way.

This is not the case with the Old Dean Forest, the legal status of which is unique, having been established by Act of Parliament in 1667. The Act requiring *'eleven thousand acres of Dean to be enclosed under protection of the Crown, with mounds and fences according to the true intent and purport of this Act.'* The purpose of the statute is clearly set out at the commencement, *'for as much as the wood and timber of the Crown which of late years was of good quality and value within the Forest of Dean in the County of Gloucestershire, is becoming totally destroyed ...'* The Act particularly prohibited the granting or obtaining of any rights within the Forest area and this Act was largely repeated by the Dean Forest (Timber) Act 1808. This again empowered the Crown to enclose eleven thousand acres, to preserve the forest growth and prevented any public rights arising. This position was changed by the Crown Estate Act of 1961, which removed the statutory restrictions on public rights arising in future.

Further complications arose from the report of the National Forest Park Committee in 1938, which permitted free public access to the Forest generally, and this has remained the policy of the Forestry Commission ever since. Outside the Dean Forest area claims for public paths to be included in the Definitive Rights of Way map, were largely frustrated by Gloucestershire County Council's vacillation on the legal issues. Where some rights of way were included in the preliminary stages, the Forestry Commission raised objections which resulted in long drawn out legal arguments. The result was an eventual compromise, with some rights of way shown on the Forest periphery and, importantly for The Gloucestershire Way, a right of way wending the length of the Old Statutory Forest.

The modern Forest of Dean is very much a mix of commercial timber production, recreational facilities and conservation. At present Forest Enterprise provide eight major picnic sites and car parks, and many smaller sites. Four camp sites are recognised internationally. In addition to family and holiday recreation, good walking is available throughout the Forest, together with more specialised activities such as rock climbing and mountain biking.

Mining and smelting of iron ore was an industry before the Roman occupation and during medieval times the Forest became the greatest iron working area in Britain. In the 17th century charcoal blast furnaces were operating throughout the Forest wherever water power was available, and by 1700, eleven of the 24 furnaces in England and Wales were situated in the Forest. The advent of steam power enabled deeper mining for both iron and highly prized coal. In the 1820s new coke furnaces were built at Parkend and Cinderford. The output of ore peaked at 199,000 tons in 1871 and iron mining finally ceased in the Forest in 1945, after a period of 2,000 years.

There are one thousand sites of industrial archaeology including medieval iron workings, Victorian coal mines and blast furnaces. Small scale coal extraction still continues as 'free miners' exploit their rights, although few give their seams such imaginative names as the 'True Blue', 'Rain Proof' or 'Gentleman Colliers' which existed in earlier years. The output of Dean Collieries in 1880 amounted to 760,000 tons, and as late as 1945 half the male population of Dean was employed in coal mining activities.

The expansion of these two industries in the 18th century brought about the widespread use of horse drawn tramways, many of which were soon converted to railways.

The Forest of Dean tram road opened in 1809 and carried as much as 20,000 tons of coal in a year, to the River Severn at Bullo Pill. Haie Tunnel on this stretch of line may well have been the earliest railway tunnel in the world. The track was relaid as 'broad gauge' in 1854 and was later reduced to standard gauge in 1872. A passenger service was in operation up to 1958. The remains of these once great industries can be seen at Dean Heritage Centre at Soudley and the Norchard Steam Centre near Lydney.

Appendix 2

Will Harvey was born at Hartbury but spent his early life at Minsterworth. At later intervals he lived in the Forest and at Gloucester. Although he trained and worked as a solicitor, he appears to have had little interest in his chosen profession, displaying a more enthusiastic aptitude for the more ethereal activities of poetry and music.

Before service in the First World War, Harvey had met Ivor Gurney, a fellow pupil at King's School, Gloucester, and they formed a close friendship bound up in their appreciation of music, literature and the Gloucestershire countryside. For a period Gurney made a virtual second home with Harvey and his parents at the Redlands, Minsterworth. The pair spent a great deal of their time walking, and sometimes carousing, but developing their deeper interest in poetry and music. Harvey never developed his talent for music as Gurney was able to, but both benefited from their association with Herbert Howells and John Haines, also to be recognised as a fine musician and a poet respectively.

Gurney's talent and the pleasure of his poetry is well accepted today. Many of his splendid songs, and over 300 poems have been published, providing a proper memorial to his qualities as a musician and poet.

Like Harvey, much of his poetry was written while serving in the squalid conditions of trench warfare. It was his misfortune to suffer ill health, with signs of mental instability early in life. Problems, no doubt, exacerbated by his experiences of war.

He continued to write memorable music and verse whilst detained in mental hospitals which enabled him to recapture his carefree love of the Gloucestershire countryside up to his early death.

Will Harvey also wrote some of his best poetry from the trenches and as a prisoner of war. On his return to Gloucestershire he resumed his profession as a solicitor. He continued to write poetry, but some of his writing reveals his frustrated literary and poetic inclinations. Nonetheless he is remembered for his poetry, much of which was published in his own collections and subsequently in many anthologies.

THE GLOUCESTERSHIRE WAY

Harvey is buried at Minsterworth and walkers who take pleasure from his poetry may care to pause at his graveside, which The Gloucestershire Way intentionally passes.

Appendix 3

The Dixton Harvesters

Two large canvases, 9 ft x 3 ft in Cheltenham Art Gallery, obviously painted from the summit of Dixton Hill looking west and east respectively. The latter is a wonderfully evocative picture of rural England, where, with artistic licence, 120 inhabitants of the parish of Alderton are shown carrying out the full cycle of haymaking. Detailed study of the painting reveals the compelling lifelikeness of the haymakers depicted. A line of mowers scythe to music, women and girls rake the hay whilst men and boys fork it into stooks. Elsewhere a piper leads men and women with rakes and forks dancing across the field whilst a lifelike line of Morris dancers gaily leap out of a corner of the picture.

This is a truly magical picture which no doubt fairly accurately records scenes of 250 years ago. However, a compelling feature is the fact that the hayfield retains the identical outline and hedgerows not only around the meadow but the adjoining fields as well. The fact that we have lost the elm tree in the last 25 years contributes to this comparison as the painting depicts an era before the elm was common in our hedgerows. A photograph reveals a scene almost identical to the painting.

Appendix 4

Tourist Information Centres

Cheltenham Spa Tourist Information Centre
Municipal Offices, 77 The Promenade, Cheltenham Spa.
01242 522878

Cirencester Tourist Information Centre
Corn Hall Market Place, Cirencester. 01285 654180

Coleford Tourist Information Centre
27 Market Place, Coleford. 01594 836307

Gloucester Tourist Information Centre
St. Michael's Tower, The Cross, Gloucester. 01452 421188

Stow-on-the-Wold Tourist Information Centre
Hollis House, The Square, Stow-on-the-Wold. 01451 831082

Tewkesbury Tourist Information Centre
The Museum, Barton Street, Tewkesbury. 01684 295027

Winchcombe Tourist Information Centre
The Town Hall, High Street, Winchcombe. 01242 602925
(Not open all year round)

Chepstow Tourist Information Centre
Castle Car Park, Bridge Street, Chepstow, Gwent. 01291 623772